STARLIGHT THROUGH THE SHADOWS

AND

Other Gleams from the King's Word

BY THE LATE
FRANCES RIDLEY HAVERGAL

"Until the day break, and the shadows flee away."—CANT. ii. 17

NEW YORK
E. P. DUTTON AND COMPANY
1882

PREFACE.

"Work for 1879, if the Lord will. To write 'Starlight through the Shadows,' a daily book for Invalids." Such was the intention of my dear sister, F. R. H. Having herself passed through the shadows of sickness and sorrow, she sought to bring some "starry promise sure," which might be more welcome, to the feeble eye, than the dazzling rays of brighter promises.

In answer to a suggestion, that she should write on some other subjects, her characteristic reply was: "I don't think I have got any real "commission to write anything at all for next "autumn, except the invalid book. I believe "I am going off the line of my especial calling "if once I begin to think of writing as a matter "of business and success and cheque, and all "that; and I can't expect the same blessing in "it.   And so, though of course it stands to rea- "son that the invalid book must have a very "limited circulation compared to the others, I "shall be much happier doing that; and I be- "lieve I shall have more real, *i. e.*, spiritual results "from it, than if I set myself to do any others, "because I do think God gave me the thought "to do this one.   I have felt so very strongly and "sweetly hitherto, that my pen was to be used "*only* for the Master, that I am very fearful of "getting the least out of the course in which I "have felt His blessing."   (*March* 1879.)

Only eleven chapters were written, when for *her* all shadows fled away, and were exchanged for the shadowless splendor of the very Light of Light !

To complete a seventh and last volume of F. R. H.'s Royal Series, selections have been made from her unpublished manuscripts.

My beloved sister's life-long interest in all missionary work seems to culminate in her "Marching Orders." By request of Mr. Eugene Stock, she wrote these papers for the *Church Missionary Gleaner* of 1879.

Outlines of addresses given at various times, with other papers, show her diligent searchings in the Scripture of truth.

May the Holy Spirit's blessing cause them to be helpful Gleams from the King's Word.

MARIA V. G. HAVERGAL.

December 14*th*, 1881.

CONTENTS.

———

		Page
STARLIGHT THROUGH THE SHADOWS:		
I.	Softly and Safely	3
II.	What seemeth Him good	10
III.	The Silence of Love	18
IV.	The Dew of the Word	23
V.	With Whom we have to do	30
VI.	Things which He suffered	36
VII.	The Lord's Cherishing	41
VIII.	Fresh Glory	46
IX.	This God is our God	51
X.	Thy Hand	58
XI.	"I pray for them"	61
MARCHING ORDERS, Nos. I. to IX.		63
OUTLINES OF ADDRESSES:		
Leprosy. Leviticus xiii.		97
Holiness, and being God's own. Lev. xx. 26		99
Christ our Law-Fulfiller. Lev. xxvii. 34		103
The Voice from the Mercy Seat. Num. vii. 89		109

viii   CONTENTS.

                                                        Page
Forgiveness. Num. xiv. 19.   114
The Brazen Serpent. Num. xxi. 8, 9   .   . 122
The Continual Burnt Offering. Num. xxviii. 3–6 . 127
Canticles i. 1–8 132
Everlasting Love   141
Everlasting Life   144
Notes of Address to Y. W. C. A. Meeting. Ps. li. 149
Notes of Address to Y. W. C. A. Meeting at
    Swansea, April 17, 1879. Hos. iii. 1–3   . 152

Miscellaneous Papers:
Sickness from God's Hand 155
Are all the Children of God?   159
Six Illustrations of the Unity in Diversity of the
    Holy Scriptures 161
Internal Evidence of the Probability that St. Paul
    wrote the Epistle to the Hebrews .   .   . 165

I.

Softly and Safely.

"I will lead on softly, according as the cattle that goeth before me and the children be able to endure."—GEN. xxxiii. 14.

THE story of Jacob's thoughtfulness for the cattle and the children is a beautiful little picture. He would not let them be overdriven even for one day. Verse 13: "My lord knoweth that the children are tender, and the flocks and herds with young are with me: and if men should overdrive them one day, all the flock will die."

He would not lead on according to what a strong man like Esau could do and expected them to do, but only according to what they were able to endure. Verse 12: "Let us take our journey, and let us go, and I will go before thee." He had had so much to do with them that he knew exactly how far they could go in a day; and he made that his only consideration in arranging the marches.

Perhaps his own halting thigh made him the more considerate for "the foot of the cattle"

and "the foot of the children" (see margin).
Besides, he had gone the same wilderness journey years before (chap. xxix. 1: "Then Jacob
went on his journey, and came into the land
of the people of the east"), when they were
not yet in existence, and knew all about its
roughness and heat and length by personal experience. And so he said, "I will lead on
softly."

"For ye have not passed this way heretofore" (Josh. iii. 4). We have not passed this
way heretofore, but the Lord Jesus has. "For
we have not an high priest which cannot be
touched with the feeling of our infirmities" (Heb.
iv. 15). It is all untrodden and unknown ground
to us, but He knows it all by personal experience;
the steep bits that take away our breath, the
stony bits that make our feet ache so, the hot
shadeless stretches that make us feel so exhausted, the rushing rivers that we have to pass
through, Jesus has gone through it all before
us. "For Himself took our infirmities and bare
our sicknesses" (Matt. viii. 17). "For in that
He Himself hath suffered being tempted" (Heb.
ii. 18). He was wearied with His journey; "Jesus therefore, being wearied with His journey"
(John iv. 6). Not some but all the many waters

went over Him, and yet did not quench His love. "All Thy waves and Thy billows are gone over me" (Ps. xlii. 7). "Many waters cannot quench love, neither can the floods drown it" (Cant. viii. 7).

He was made a perfect Leader by the things which He suffered. Heb. ii. 10: "To make the Captain of their salvation perfect through sufferings." Heb. v. 8, 9: "Though He were a Son, yet learned He obedience by the things which He suffered; and being made perfect, He became the Author of eternal salvation unto all them that obey Him." For now He knows all about it, and leads us softly according as we are able to endure.

"For He knoweth our frame" (Ps. ciii. 14). And He does not only know, with that sort of up-on-the-shelf knowledge which is often guilty of want of thought among ourselves, but He *remembereth* that we are dust. Ps. lxxviii. 39: "For He remembered that they were but flesh." Think of that when you are tempted to question the gentleness of the leading. He is remembering all the time; and not one step will He make you take beyond what your foot is able to endure. Never mind if you think it will not be able for the step that seems to come next;

either He will so strengthen it that it shall be able, or He will call a sudden halt, and you shall not have to take it at all.

Is it not restful to know that you are not answerable to any Esaus, for how much you get through, or how far you are led on in the day! "They" don't know, or, knowing, don't remember, the weakness or the drawbacks. Maybe they wonder you do not get on farther and faster, doing the work better, bearing up against the suffering or the sorrow more bravely. And maybe you feel wounded and wearied without a word being said, simply because you know they *don't* know! Then turn to the Good Shepherd in whose "feeble flock" you are, and remember that He remembers. Talk to Him about it; and if too weary even for that, then just lean on Him with whom you have to do. For "all things are naked and opened unto the eyes of Him with whom we have to do" (Heb. iv. 13). It is only when we are coming up from the wilderness, leaning on our Beloved, that we can realize how softly He is leading us. "Who is this that cometh up from the wilderness, leaning upon her Beloved?" (Cant. viii. 5.) For if we are pulling this way and that way, straggling and struggling and wasting our steps by little turnings aside, He may have to resort to other means to keep us in the way at all. But if we are willing to lean, we shall soon find that He is leading not only rightly (that we never doubted), but softly too. And leading softly will not be leading slowly. "And He led them forth by the right way" (Ps. cvii. 7).

Minds are differently constituted, and some do not readily grasp as a real promise what is indicated in a figure. But if the figure is a true illustration, we are sure to find the same promise somewhere else in a direct form. So if you hesitate to appropriate the promise that Jesus as your Good Shepherd "will lead on softly," take the same thing from that familiar verse in Isa. xl.; "shall gently lead" is the very same word in the original; and in the dear old 23rd Psalm "He leadeth me" is still the same word, and might be read, "He gently, or softly, leadeth me." These are the true sayings of your God.

One sees at a glance, by referring to a Concordance, the touching fact that our Leader Himself experienced very different leading. Never once was He gently led. He was led into the wilderness to be tempted of the devil (Matt. iv. 1); He was led by men filled with wrath to the brow of the hill, that they might cast Him down

headlong (Luke iv. 19); He was led away to
Annas, led away to Caiaphas (John xviii. 13,
Matt. xxvi. 57); led into the council of the
elders and chief priests and scribes (Luke xxii.
66); led to Pontius Pilate (Matt. xxvii. 2),
and into the hall of judgment (John xviii. 28).
And then He, our Lord Jesus Christ, was led
as a sheep to the slaughter (Acts viii. 32); led
away to be crucified! (John xix. 16.) Verily,
"His way was much rougher and darker than
mine."

That is how Jesus was led. But as for His
people, "He guided them in the wilderness
like a flock, and He led them on safely, so that
they feared not" (Ps. lxxviii. 52, 53).

Not only safely as to the end of the journey,
but as to each step. For He employs another
figure to prove this; saying that He led them
"as a horse in the wilderness, that they should
not stumble."*   "As a beast goeth down into

---

* This exposition of the passage is familiar and obvious
enough; but I was much interested by a friend's calling
my attention to the French translation, which brings it
out beautifully: "L'Esprit de l'Eternel les a conduits
tout doucement, comme on conduit une bête qui descend
dans une plaine. C'est ainsi que Tu as conduit Ton
peuple."

the valley, the Spirit of the Lord caused him to rest." Can you not see the steep stony path of the rocky descent into a desert valley, and the careful owner's hand leading the hesitating horse, keeping fast hold of his head, and encouraging him with tones which he can understand, till the halting place at the bottom is safely reached! "So didst Thou lead Thy people," says Isaiah. So He leadeth me! responds your heart, does it not? Softly and safely, step by step, and mile by mile, till the desert journey is over and the Father's home reached!

Then trust Him for to-day
　As thine unfailing Friend,
And let Him lead thee all the way
　Who loveth to the end.
And let the morrow rest
　In His belovèd hand,
His good is better than our best,
　As we shall understand;
If, trusting Him who faileth never,
We rest on Him to-day, for ever!

II.

What Seemeth Him Good.

"Let Him do what seemeth Him good."
I Sam. iii. 18.

ELI spoke these words under the terrible certainty of heavy judgments upon his house,
because the Lord had spoken it.   But how often
God's dear children tremble to say an unre-
served "*Let* Him do what seemeth Him good,"
though they are under no such shadow of certainly coming events !   It is almost easier to say
it when a crushing blow has actually fallen, than
when there is suspense and uncertainty as to
what the Lord may be going to do.   There is
always more or less of this element of suspense
and uncertainty.   One can hardly imagine a life
in which there are no clouds, little or great, within the horizon, even when the sky is clearest
over head.   We hold not a treasure on earth
which we are sure of keeping; and we never
know whether gain or loss, failure or success,
ease or pain, lies before us.   And if we were
allowed to put our finger on the balance of un-

certainties and turn it as we chose, we should be sure to defeat some ultimate aim by securing a nearer one, and prevent some greater good by grasping a lesser. I think if we were permitted to try such an experiment, we should soon grow utterly puzzled and weary, and find ourselves landed in complications of mistakes; and if we had any sense left, we should want to put it all back into our Father's hands, and say "Let Him do what seemeth *Him* good," then we should feel relieved and at rest.

Then why not be relieved and at rest at once? For "it is *the Lord*," who is going to do we know not what. That is a volume in itself,— the Lord who loves you, the Lord who thinks about you and cares for you, the Lord who understands you, the Lord who never makes a mistake, the Lord who spared not His own Son but gave Him up for you! Will you not let *Him* do what seemeth Him good? Then think *what* it is you are to let Him do. Something out of your sight, perhaps, but not out of His sight. For the original word in every case is "what is good *in His eyes*." Those Eyes see through and through, and all round and beyond everything. So what is good in His Eyes must be absolutely and entirely good, a vast deal better than our

best!   There is great rest in knowing that He
will do what is *right*, but He crowns the right-
ness with the goodness; and when we see this,
the rest is crowned with gladness.   Ought it,
then, to be so very hard to say, "Let Him do
what seemeth Him *good*"?

It is very interesting to trace out that in each
recorded instance of this expression of submissive trust at a juncture of dark uncertainty
the result was always something most evidently
"good," in the eyes of those who ventured to
say it.

First, there were the Gibeonites.   They came
to Joshua (who by his very name, as well as
office, was a direct type of Christ), "sore afraid
for their lives."   But, because he had made peace
with them, they said, "Behold, we are in thine
hand : as it seemeth good and right unto thee
to do unto us, do."   A beautiful illustration of
confidence based upon covenant.   Now see how
their trust was justified.   "*So* did he unto them,"
that is, as it was good and right in his eyes;
and the first thing was, that he "delivered
them out of the hand of the children of Israel
that they slew them not."   And the next thing
was his ascending from Gilgal to fight their bat-
tles for them, conquering five kings for them,

and calling upon the sun to stand still over their city "about a whole day," so that "there was no day like that before it, or after it."

Next we find the children of Israel sold for their evil deeds, into the hands of the Philistines and Ammonites, and vexed and oppressed for eighteen years. ("Vexed and oppressed,"—does that describe your case?) They come to the Lord with bare, excuseless confession, "We have sinned," and then they cast themselves on bare undeserved mercy: "Do thou unto us whatsoever seemeth good unto Thee." And what then? "His soul was grieved for the misery of Israel." Could anything be more humanly tender, as well as Divinely magnanimous! Is it not a lesson to come straight to His heart with any misery of which the sting is that we have brought it on ourselves, and deserved it a thousand-fold? First confess the sin, and then leave the sorrows wholly in His hands, and we find Him verily "the same Lord, whose property is always to have mercy." And mercy includes help, for the Lord did not stop short at grieving over their misery; He sent Jephthah to deliver them, so that they "dwelled safe" for about thirty years. (Compare Judges xi. 33 and 1 Sam. xii. 11.)

Now turn to 1 Chron. xix. 13, "and let the Lord do that which is good in His sight." Here Joab finds a double army "set against him before and behind." He makes the wisest arrangements he can think of, and encourages his brother, and then he says, "and let the Lord do that which is good in His sight." And what the Lord did was to give him a splendid victory. It does not seem that he had to fight or suffer any loss at all; the Syrians and Ammonites simply fled before him : verses 15, 16. "And when the children of Ammon saw that the Syrians were fled, they likewise fled before Abishai his brother, and entered into the city. Then Joab came to Jerusalem. And when the Syrians saw that they were put to the worse before Israel, they sent messengers and drew forth the Syrians that were beyond the river."

The most touching instance however is David. "And the king said unto Zadok, carry back the ark of God into the city : if I shall find favor in the eyes of the Lord, He will bring me again and show me both it and His habitation. But if He thus say, I have no delight in thee; behold here am I, let Him do to me as seemeth good unto Him." Driven from his royal home by his own son, passing amid tears over the brook

Kidron, going toward the way of the wilderness, "weary and weak handed," the wisest head in the land giving counsel against him, and the hearts of the men of Israel going after the traitor, and now losing the visible token of the presence of God Himself! I do not see how any of us could be brought to such a pass as all this! And yet he said, "Let Him do to me as seemeth good unto Him." But only a little while, and the Lord, whom he trusted so implicitly in such depths, restored to him all that seemed so nearly lost, and raised him again to royal heights of prosperity and praise.

Did not these things happen unto them for ensamples? If they, in the dim old days of type and veil, could so trust the God of Israel, should we, who have the light of the knowledge of the glory of God in the face of Jesus Christ, hesitate to utter the same expression of submissive confidence? And if He has caused such records of His gracious responses to their submission to be written, should we not take them as intended to encourage our hearts in the gloomy and dark day? See now if you cannot find something like your own case in one or other of them, and remember you have the same Saviour and the same Lord to do with. And then, venture the word!

Just *let* Him do what seemeth Him good, and tell Him so! It may be you have been actually hindering deliverance and thwarting help, by not "letting" Him. Do not say "But what difference can that make? He will do what He pleases, of course, whether I am willing or not." Not exactly that. Does it make no difference if the patient quietly lets the surgeon do what he thinks best? A remedy applied by force, or submitted to unwillingly, may be quite counteracted by fidget, or by feverishness induced or increased through setting one's self against what is prescribed or advised. The Lord's remedies do not have fair play, when we set ourselves against them. Even Omnipotence waits for the faith that will *let* it act.

"And the vessel that he made of clay was marred in the hand of the potter. So he made it again another vessel, as seemed good to the potter to make it." See Jer. xviii. 4.

If the "vessel made of clay," that was marred in the hand of the potter, could have resisted that skilful hand, how would he have been able to make it again another vessel, as it seemed good to him to make it? The unresisting clay could not help *letting* the potter remould it, into a better and permanent form; but we *can* hinder, simply by not "letting." But will you do this? For "now, O Lord, Thou art our Father, we are the clay, and Thou our Potter." Whatever may be our Potter's mysterious mouldings, or our Father's mysterious dealings (I do not mean abstract, or possible, or future; but real, and present, and pressing), let us give the one sweet answer which meets *everything:* "even so, Father, for so it seemed good in Thy sight."

> Not yet thou knowest what I do
>   Within thine own weak breast;
> To mould thee to My image true,
>   And fit thee for My rest.
> But yield thee to my loving skill;
>   The veilèd work of grace,
> From day to day progressing still,
>   It is not thine to trace.
>
> Yes, walk by faith and not by sight,
>   Fast clinging to My hand;
> Content to feel My love and might,
>   Not yet to understand.
> A little while thy course pursue,
>   Till grace to glory grow;
> *Then* what I am, and *what I do*,
>   Hereafter thou shalt know.
>
>   (*Ministry of Song*).

III.

The Silence of Love.

"Rest in (*margin* 'Be silent to') the Lord."
PSALM xxxvii. 7.

AN invalid was left alone one evening for a little while. After many days of acute pain there was a lull. "Now," she thought, "I shall be able to pray a little." But she was too wearied out and exhausted for this; feeling that utter weakness of mind and body which cannot be realized without actual experience, when the very lips shrink from the exertion of a whisper, and it seems too much effort of thought to shape even unspoken words. Only one whisper came: "Lord Jesus, I am so tired!" She prayed no more; she could not frame even a petition that, as she could not speak to Him, He would speak to her. But the Lord Jesus knew all the rest; He knew how she had waited for and wanted the sweet conscious communing with Him, the literal talking to Him and telling Him all that was in her heart. And He knew that, although a quiet and comparatively painless hour had come, she was "so tired" that she could not think. Very tenderly did He, who knows how to speak a word in season to the weary, choose a message in reply to that little whisper. "Be silent to the Lord!" It came like a mother's "hush" to one whom his mother comforteth. It was quite enough, as every Spirit-given word is; and the acquiescent silence was filled with perfect peace. Only real friends understand silence. With a passing guest or ceremonial acquaintance you feel under an obligation to talk; you make effort to entertain them as a matter of courtesy; you may be tired or weak, but no matter, you feel you must exert yourself. But with a very dear and intimate friend sitting by you, there is no feeling of the kind. To be sure, you may talk if you feel able: pouring out all sort of confidences, relieved and refreshed by the interchange of thoughts and sympathies. But if you are very tired, you know you do not need to say a word. You are perfectly understood, and you know it. You can enjoy the mere fact of your friend's presence, and find that does you more good than conversation. The sense of that present and sympathetic affection rests you more than any words. And your friend takes it as the

highest proof of your friendship and confidence
and probably never loves you so vividly as in
these still moments.   No matter that twilight is
falling, and that you cannot see each other's
faces, the presence and the silence are full of
brightness and eloquence, and you feel they are
enough.

Even so we may be silent to the Lord.   Just
because we know He loves us so really and
understands us so thoroughly!   There is no
need when very weary, bodily or mentally, or
both, to force ourselves to entertain Him, so to
speak; to go through a sort of duty-work of a
certain amount of uttered words or arranged
thoughts.   That might be if He were only to
us as a wayfaring man that turneth aside to
tarry for a night, but not with the beloved and
Gracious One who has come in to abide with
us, and is always there!   If this is His relation
to us, there is no fear but what there will be, at
other times, plenty of intercourse; but now, when
we are "so tired," we may just be silent to Him
instead of speaking to Him.

This is one of the expressions which are ex
clusively used concerning the things of God
There is no such thing as being silent to any
one else. Silent *with* a mortal friend, but never

silent *to* any but the Immortal One.   Though it
has its earthly analogy, it is not identically the
same.   For none but our Lord can interpret
the unseen pulsings of that which to human
ken is *only* silence.   He hears the music they
are measuring out before Him.   He takes the
confidence of that hush at its full value of golden
love.   He sees the soul's attitude of devotion
and faith through the shadows which hide it from
itself.

Sometimes He takes the opportunity of our
silence to speak Himself.   He answers it "with
good words and comfortable words."   And do
we not know that one such word from Him is
more than anything else, worth ten thousand-
fold all the weariness or exhaustion of pain which
brought us to be silent !

But sometimes He answers silence with silence.
What then ?   Are we to conclude that He is
gone away, or is not thinking about us, for-
getting to be gracious?   We are judging Him
as He would not judge us.   He did not put
such an interpretation on our silence; then why
should we on His ?   Let us take His interpretation of it; surely we should believe what He
Himself asserts !   "He will be silent in His
love" (Zeph. iii. 17, *margin*).   Can any words

be more beautiful ! It is as if He, even He,
who made man's mouth, had made no words
which could express His exceeding great love,
and therefore He could only expand it in the
silence which lies above and below and beyond
all language. When we have said, as very likely
we have often done, "Why art Thou silent unto
me, O Lord?" why did we not take His own ex
quisite answer, and trust the love that was veiled
in the silence? For whenever we can say, "Tru
ly my soul waiteth upon (*Heb.* is silent to) God,"
we may rest assured that any apparent waiting on
His part is only "that He may be gracious," yes
"*very* gracious unto thee."

We may be sure He has many things to say
to us, when He sees we can bear them. But
till His time to speak is come, let our silence of
trust respond to His silence of love.

IV.

The Dew of the Word.

"My speech shall distil as the dew."—DEUT. xxxii. 2.

BUT who hears the dew fall? What microphone could reveal that music to our "gross unpurgèd ears"?

The dew distils · in silence. So does the speech of our God. Most frequently in the silence of trust already spoken of. In that stillness God's silent love can be condensed into dewlike communications; not read, not heard, but made known by the direct power of the Spirit upon the soul.

Most often He does this by thrilling into remembrance something from the written Word, already learnt, but now flashing out in the quickened memory as if it had never been heard before.

We do not get much of this if we are always in the midst of noise and turmoil and bustle. He can, and now and then He does, send this "speech" through a very chaos of bustle or trouble. He can make a point of silence in the

very centre of a cyclone, and speak there to our
hearts.   But the more usual way is to make a
wider silence for His dew to fall, by calling us
apart into some quiet place of sorrow or sickness.   So when we find ourselves thus led into
a wilderness, let us forthwith look out for the
dew, and it will not fail.   Then our desert will
rejoice and blossom as the rose; very likely
much more so than the hot harvest fields, or the
neat gardens from which we have been called
away.

The dew distils in darkness.   Not in the
darkness of external trial alone.   It is easy to
understand that, and most of us have experienced it.   The beautiful thing is that the life-
giving speech distils even in soul darkness.
"Who is among you that feareth the Lord, that
walketh in darkness and hath no light?   Let
him trust in the name of the Lord, and stay
himself upon his God."   There are times when
we simply cannot see anything, when there is
nothing for it but to hold on and trust in the
dark; times when we do not seem even to be
walking in the dark, but when, like Micah, we
"*sit* in darkness," too feeble even to grope.
Such darkness often comes in a time of re-
action and weariness after special work and

exertion, very often indeed after great or exciting success, sometimes even after unusually vivid spiritual blessing. An interval of convalescence after acute illness, when the overtaxed nervous energy has more than it can do in slowly refilling the chalice of life that had been so nearly "spilled on the ground," is peculiarly liable to it. And the sufferers who never pass beyond that stage, who are never any more than "a *little* better," know its shadow perhaps best of all. It does not say so, but I think the Lord Jesus must have known it, because He was made like unto us in all things, and submitted not only to the causes but to the effects of all the natural experiences of the nature which He took on Him.

Now it seems to me that it is in this kind of darkness that His speech distils as the dew. You look out some dark night after a hot dusty day; there is no storm, no rain, there is not the least token to your senses of what is going on. You look out again in the morning, and you see every blade and leaf tipped with a dewdrop; everything is revived and freshened, prepared for the heat of the day, and smiling at the glow. Just so His words are silently falling on your souls in the darkness, and preparing them for the day. They do not come with any sensible power, nothing flashes out from the page as at other times, nothing shines so as to shed any pleasant light on your path, you do not hear any sound of abundance of rain. You seem as if you could not take the words in; and if you could, your mind is too weary to meditate on them. But they are distilling as the dew all the time!

Do not quarrel with the invisible dew because it is not a visible shower. The Lord would send a shower if that was the true need to be supplied to His vineyard; but as He is sending His speech in another form, you may be quite sure it is because He is supplying your true need thereby. You cannot see why it is so, and I do not pretend to explain; but what does that matter! He knows which way to water His vineyard. These words of His, which you are remembering so feebly, or reading without being able to grasp, are not going to return void. They are doing His own work on your soul, only in quite a different way to what you would choose. By and by they will sparkle out in the light of a new morning, and you will find yourself starting fresh, and perhaps wondering how it is that the leaves of life which hung

so limp and drooping are so fresh and firm
again on their stems. This also cometh forth
from the Lord of hosts, which is wonderful in
counsel, and excellent in working.

The dew falls not in one mass of water, but
innumerable little drops. What one drop does
not reach another does. So it is not one over-
whelmingly powerful word which does this holy
night work in the soul, but the unrealized influence of many, dropping softly on the plants of
the Lord which He has planted, one resting
here, another there; oue touching an unrecog-
nised need, and another reaching an unconsciously failing grace. "Each drop uncounted
hath its own mission, and is duly sent to its own
leaf or blade."

Sometimes God's dew goes on falling through
many hours of the night. The watches seem
very long, and the starlight does not reveal it.
But none of it is lost; some is already doing a
hidden work as it falls around the very roots of
our being, and some is ready to be revealed in
sparkling brightness when the night is over,
lessons learnt among the shadows to be lived
out in the sunshine.

The object of the dew is to maintain life in
dry places and seasons. Dwellers in rainless

regions understand this better than we do, but
we can see enough of it in any dry week in
summer to understand the beauty of the figure.
.So this speech is spirit and life to souls which
are, however feebly, yet really alive unto God.
Dew does nothing for the stones. You would
not know there ever was any at all if you only
look at the gravel path. And it makes no difference at all to a dead leaf. But it falls on
the little fading plant that could hardly have
lived through many more days of July sunshine,
the weak little stem straightens up as the leaves
absorb the life-renewing moisture, and the closed
blossom can open out again with fresher fragrance than before. So God keeps on distilling
His speech into our frail spiritual life, or it
would soon wither up. Dryness is more to be
dreaded than darkness.

Only let us be trustfully content to let this
dew of heaven fall in the dark, and when we
cannot hear or see, recollect that He says, " My
speech shall distil as the dew." Our part is to
believe this, and leave ourselves open to it as
we read what perhaps seems a very dim page
of the Bible with very tired eyes; or, perhaps,
lie still through the long hours of a literal night,
with no power to meditate on the fitful gleams

of half recollected verses that just cross our minds and seem to leave no trace. Never mind, the dew is falling !

Softly the dew in the evening descends,
   Cooling the sun-heated ground and the gale;
Flow'rets all fainting it soothingly tends,
   Ere the consumings of mid-day prevail.
Sweet gentle dewdrops, how mystic your fall,
Wisdom and mercy float down in you all.

Softer and sweeter by far is that Dew
   Which from the Fountain of Comfort distils,
When the worn heart is created anew,
   And hallowed pleasure its emptiness fills.
Lord, let Thy Spirit be-dew my dry fleece !
Faith then shall triumph, and trouble shall cease.

       (*Rev. W. H. Havergal: last hymn*, 1870.)

V.

With whom we have to do.

"Him with whom we have to do."—Heb. iv. 13.

THERE are wonderful depths of comfort in
these words. I cannot fathom them for
you. I only want to guide you to look where
the deep places are, asking the Holy Spirit to
put a long sounding line into your hand, that
you may prove for yourself how great is the
depth.

These words seem to meet every sort of need
of comfort. If it is perplexity, or oppressive
puzzle what to do, when we cannot see through
things,—or if it is being unable to explain yourself to others, and trials or complications arising
out of this: just fall back upon "Him with
whom we have to do," to whose eyes all things
are naked and opened. He is your Guide,—
why need you puzzle? He is your Shield,—why
need you try so hard or wish so much to explain
and vindicate yourself?

If it is sense of *sin* which does not let you be
comfortable, turn *at once* to " Him with whom

you have to do." Remember, it is not with
Satan that you have to do, nor with your
accusing conscience, but with Jesus. He will
deal with all the rest; you only have to deal
with Him. And He is your great High Priest.
He has made full Atonement for you; for the
very sins that are weighing on you now. The
blood of that Atonement, His own precious
blood, cleanseth us from all sin. Cleanseth
whom? People that have not sinned? People
that don't want to be cleansed? Thank God
for the word "cleanseth *us*," us who have sinned
and who want to be cleansed. And you have
to do with Him who shed it for your cleansing,
who His own self bare your sins in His own
body on the tree.

If it is *temptation* that will not let you rest,
come straight away out of the very thick of it;
it may be with the fiery darts sticking in you.
Come with all the haunting thoughts that you
hate, just as you are, to "Him with whom you
have to do." You would not or could not tell
the temptations to any one else; but then you
have not got to do with any one else in the
matter, but *only* with Jesus. And He "suffered,
being tempted." The very fact that you are
distressed by the temptation proves that it *is*

temptation, and that you have a singular claim
on the sympathy of our tempted Lord, a claim
which He most tenderly acknowledges. But
use it instantly; don't creep, but *flee* unto Him
to hide you from the assaults which you are too
weak to meet.

If it is *bodily weakness, sickness, or pain,* how
very sweet it is to know that we have to do
with Jesus, who is "touched with the feeling of
our infirmities." (The word is the same that is
elsewhere translated sickness: John xi. 2–4.)
Don't you sometimes find it very hard to make
even your doctor understand *what* the pain is
like? Words don't seem to convey it. And
after you have explained the trying and weary-
ing sensation as best you can, you are convinced
those who have not felt it do not understand it.

Now think of Jesus not merely entering into
the fact, but into the feeling, of what you are
going through. "Touched with the *feeling*"—
how deep that goes! When we turn away to
Him in our wordless weariness of pain which
only He understands, we find out that we have to
do with Him in quite a different sense from how
we have to do with any one else. We could not
do without Him, and thank God we shall never
have to do without Him.

Why enumerate other shadows which this same soft light can enter and dispel? They may be cast by any imaginable or unimaginable shape of trouble or need, but the same light rises for them all, if we will only turn towards the brightness of its rising. For Jesus is He "with whom we have to do" in *every thing*, nothing can be outside of this, unless we wilfully decline to have to do with Him in it, or unbelievingly choose to have to do with "lords many."

And we are answerable only to Him in every thing; for this is included in having to do with Him. To our own Master we stand or fall; and that latter alternative is instantly put out of the question, the apostle adding, "Yea, he shall be holden up, for God is able to make him stand," *i.e.*, he who is his "own Master's" servant. To Him we have to give account, if from Him we take our orders.

We have to do with Him *directly*. So directly that it is difficult at first to grasp the directness. There is absolutely nothing between the soul and Jesus, if we will but have it so. We have Himself as our Mediator with God, and the very characteristic of a mediator is, as Job says, "that he might lay his hand

upon us both"; so the hand of Jesus, who is
Himself "the Man of Thy right hand," is laid
upon us with no intermediate link and no in-
tervening distance.   We do not need any paper
and print, let alone any human voice, between
us and Himself.

> "To Thee, O dear, dear Saviour,
>   My spirit turns for rest."

That turning is instinctive and instantaneous
when we have once learnt what it is to have
direct and personal dealing with the Lord Jesus
Christ.   Life is altogether a different thing then,
whether shady or sunshiny, and a stranger inter-
meddleth not with our hidden joy.   Perhaps
it is just this that makes such a strangely felt
difference between those who equally profess
and call themselves Christians.   Is Jesus to us
"*Him with whom we have to do*"? or is He only
Him whom we know about, and believe about,
and with whose laws and ordinances we have to
do?   This makes all the difference, and every
one who has this personal dealing with Him
knows it, and cannot help knowing it.

Do not let this discourage any one who cannot yet say "Him with whom *I* have to do."
For He is more ready and willing thus to have

to do with you, than you with Him.   You may
enter at once into this most sweet and solemn
position.   He is there already: He only waits for
you to come into it.   Only bring Him your sins
and your sinful self, ''waiting not to rid your
soul of one dark blot." Nothing else separates
between you and Him, and He will take them
all away and receive you graciously; and then you
too shall know the sacred and secret blessedness
of having to do with Jesus.

> I could not do without Thee,
>   O Jesus, Saviour dear !
> E'en when my eyes are holden,
>   I know that Thou art near.
> How dreary and how lonely
>   This changeful life would be,
> Without the sweet communion,
>   The secret rest with Thee.
>
> I could not do without Thee !
>   No other friend can read
> The spirit's strange deep longings,
>   Interpreting its need.
> No human heart can enter
>   Each deep recess of mine,
> And soothe and hush and calm it,
>   O blessèd Lord, but Thine !

VI.

Things which He Suffered.

"The things which He suffered."—Heb. v. 8.

IF we have some dear one gone before, who "suffered many things," there is neither comfort nor help to be had by dwelling on them. It would be a poor comforter who reminded you of them, and brought them back in detail to your scarred memory. One would rather do one's utmost to turn your thoughts away from them, leading you to dwell only on the present bliss, and one would fain blot out your painful remembrance of a past which it does no good to recall.

Not so does our Divine Comforter work. When He takes of the things of Christ and shows them to us, we feel that the things which He suffered are precious exceedingly, and the Spirit-wrought remembrance of them powerful beyond all else.

These "things" are only past in act, not in effect. For He was wounded for our transgressions and bruised for our iniquities of this day; the chastisement of the peace of this hour was upon Him; and though the whole head may be sick and the whole heart faint, the stripes that fell on Him are full of fresh power to heal at this moment.

> "Thy sin of *this* day
> In its shadow lay
> Between My face and One turned away."

Greater love hath no man than this, that a man lay down his life for his friends; yet that was only one of the things which he suffered, only the full stop at the close of the great charter of suffering love.

This pathetic plural is full of suggestion. How much suffering is dimly hinted in the one intimation that He bare our sicknesses! How much may be hidden under the supposition of the Jews that He was nearly fifty years of age, when so little beyond thirty! How sharp must have been the experiences which graved such lines upon the visage so marred more than any man! Think of all that must have gone on under the surface of His home life, where neither did His brethren believe in Him. Consider Him that endured such contradiction of sinners against Himself. Think what tempta-

tion must have been to the Holy One, and what
the concentration of malice and great rage when
the prince of darkness went forth to do his
worst against the lonely Son of Man, whom he
knew to be the Son of God. Think of Jesus
alone with Satan! Oh, what things He suffered
before He came to the agony and bloody sweat,
the cross and passion, which filled up the cup
which His Father gave Him to drink for us
men and for our salvation!

All this true! all this real! all this for us!

All this, that He might be made a perfect
Saviour, having learnt by personal experience
the suffering from which He saves as well as the
suffering in which He supports and with which
He sympathises, having learnt by personal experience the obedience by which "many shall
be made righteous," and which is at once our
justification and our example.

All this, that He might be a perfect Captain
of our salvation, knowing all and far more than
all the hardships of the rank and file.

All this, that He might be the Author of
eternal salvation to them that obey Him, to you
and me!

"The things which He suffered." The remembrance must touch our gratitude and love,

if anything will.   If when we looked back on some terrible suffering unto death of one who loved us dearly, suppose an elder brother, I really do not know how any heart could bear it, if we distinctly knew that all that prolonged agony was borne instead of us, and borne for nothing in the world but for love of us.   But if to this were added the knowledge that we had behaved abominably to that dying brother, done all sorts of things, now beyond recall, to grieve and vex him, not cared one bit about his love or made him any return of even natural affection, held aloof from him and sided with those who were against him; and *then* the terrible details of his slow agony were told, nay *shown* to us,—well, imagine our remorse if you can, I cannot!   The burden of grief and gratitude would be crushing, and if there were still any possible way in which we could show that poor, late gratitude, we should take it at any cost, or rather, we should count nothing at any cost if we might but prove our tardy love.   Only I think we should never know another hour's rest. But it is part of the strange power of the re-membrance of our Lord's sufferings that it brings strength and solace and peace; for, as Bunyan says, "He hath given us rest by His sorrow."

The bitterness of death to Him is the very
fountain of the sweetness of life to us.   Do the
words after all seem to fall without power or
reality on your heart?   Is it nothing, or very
little more than nothing, to you ?   Not that you
do not know it is all true, but your heart seems
cold, and your apprehension mechanical, and
your faith paralyzed;—does this describe you ?
Thank God that feelings do not alter facts !   He
suffered for this sinful coldness as well as for all
other sins.   He suffered, the Just for the unjust;
and are we not emphatically unjust when we
requite His tremendous love this way ?   Still
you don't feel it, though you own it.   You see it
all, but it is through a transparent wall of ice.
What is to be done ?   Ask, and ask at once, for
the Holy Spirit, that He may melt the ice and
take of these things of Christ, showing them to
you, not in the light of natural understanding
and mere mental reception of undeniable facts,
but revealing them with His own Divine power
and bowing your whole soul under the weight of
the exceeding great love of our Master and only
Saviour Jesus Christ, as manifested in "the
things which He suffered."   "For every one
that asketh receiveth."

VII.

The Lord's Cherishing.

"Cherisheth it."—EPH. v. 29.

"CHERISHETH it, even as the Lord the church." The church is not only "one body," but also "many members"; "for the body is not one member, but many." And what is true for the whole is true also for the smallest part. Lest any one should think the individual is rather lost in the great whole, the gracious word of our God comes down to meet the possible or passing tremor, and says: "Ye are," not only the body of Christ, but "members in particular."

Do not hesitate to take all the revelation of love that shines softly through this one word "cherisheth," for your own self; for the more you feel yourself to be the weakest imaginable member of Christ, unworthy to be a member at all of His glorious body, the more closely and sweetly will it apply to you.

For it necessarily implies, on the one side, weakness and inferiority and need. It would be nothing to us if we felt extremely strong and capable and self-contained. The Lord would never have taken the trouble to cause it to be written for such people. They would neither want it nor thank Him for it. We do not talk about "cherishing" an oak tree, or an athlete, or even a "strong minded woman." Our heart-welcome to this beautiful word, and our sense of its preciousness, will be just in proportion to our sense of being among the Lord's little ones, or weak ones, no matter what others suppose us to be. After all, are not even those who are chasing thousands, but little ones? and those who are slaying Goliaths, but weak ones? in their real and hidden relationship to their own great and mighty Saviour and Lord. Even a father in Christ or a mother in Israel may turn with the heart of a little child, lovingly and gratefully, and perhaps very wearily too, to their cherishing Lord, to be comforted afresh with the old comforts, and hushed to rest on the little pillow of some very familiar text.

The Lord Jesus has said of all who love Him, "I will love him and will manifest Myself to him." See how He manifested Himself to you in these words, as your Cherisher. The word conveys, on His side, nothing but affection, and gentle thoughtful care. How do we cherish a little weak plant? There were plenty of handsomer ones, but this little cutting or seedling was perhaps a gift in the first place; and then we took a fancy to it, so that we cared doubly for it. Then we felt a sort of pity for it, because it was such a delicate little thing; so we shielded it, and perhaps re-potted it, that it might strike its little roots more freely. We watched it day by day, giving it just enough water and not too much. We set it in the light when it was ready, and turned it round now and then, so that even too much light might not make it grow onesidedly. And when at last it put out a flower for us, we thought more of that than of any ninety-nine blossoms in the great garden. Is not this something like our Lord's cherishing?

Then think how "a nurse cherisheth her children" (1 Thess. ii. 7). That is, a "gentle" and wise one. How the little ailments are watched and attended to; how the little weary heads are laid on her shoulders and stroked to sleep; how the little meals are regulated and given; *never* forgotten,—who ever heard of such a thing ! How the little garments are kept clean and comfortable, changed and mended, as need may be. How the nursery fire is looked after (while all the while the guard is kept on the bars), so that the room should not be too hot or too cold. How the little bodies are cared for and loved every inch, even the little fingers and toes ! How the little fancies are borne with and entered into, not unheeded or scorned; and the silly little questions patiently answered, and the baby lessons taught, and the small tempers managed, and checked, and forgiven ! That is cherishing. Need we trace its close resemblance to the dealings of our infinitely patient and gentle Lord ?

Then think of the still higher and closer cherishing of the weak wife by the strong husband,—itself shown by the only possible stronger figure, "No man ever yet hated *his own flesh*, but nourisheth and cherisheth it"; this set forth by the Holy Ghost through the pen of an apostle, to convey to *you* some dim idea of the Lord's love and care and thought for *you.* What could He say more? For even thus the Lord cherisheth you,—He gives you His name to bear as your honor, and His very heart to dwell in as the home of your soul. He gives you the right of constant access, the right of continual dwelling in His presence. He makes you partaker of His very nature, joining you unto Himself, not only in a perpetual covenant, but as "one spirit" with Him. He pays all your debts, and now all your wants lie upon Him, and these wants are each and all foreseen and provided for, and supplied with untiring love. He knows in an instant when you are weary or ailing, whether in body or spirit, and knows how to speak the right word for either, speaking verily to your heart,—knows, too, when to be silent for a little while. His cherishing goes on night and day,— just as much in the dark as in the light; and will go on, faithfully, ceaselessly, all through your life-long need of it, unto the end; and there is no shadowing whisper to fall upon this life-long manifestation of love, no such word as "till death us do part." No absence of your Lord shall deprive you of it; and all that death can do is to take away the last veil, that you may see face to face, and know even as you are known. His care over you will then be exchanged for perfect joy over you. "He shall see of the travail of His soul and be satisfied."

"From glory unto glory." Though tribulation fall,
It cannot touch our treasure when Christ is all in all !
Whatever lies before us, there can be nought to fear,
For what are pain and sorrow *when Jesus Christ is near?*

VIII.

𝔉𝔯𝔢𝔰𝔥 𝔊𝔩𝔬𝔯𝔶.

"My glory was fresh in me."—JOB xxix. 20.

WHO does not know the longing for freshness! Fresh air, fresh water, fresh
flowers, the freshness of children, and of some
people's conversation and writings,—all illustrate
or lead up to that spiritual freshness which is
both pleasure and power. For it was when
Job's glory was fresh in him, that his bow was
renewed in his hand. Freshness and glory!
and yet the brilliant music of such words is
brought down to a minor strain by one little
touch—it "*was*," not "*it is*"; a melancholy
Past instead of a bright Present. Now, instead
of saddening ourselves unnecessarily by sighing,
"Ah, yes! that is always the way," let us see
how we may personally prove that it is *not*
always the way, and that Job's confessedly ex-
ceptional experience need not, and ought not,
to be ours.

First of all, if our glory is to be fresh in us, it
all depends upon what the glory in us is. If it is

any sort of our own—anything connected with that which decayeth and waxeth old in us or passeth away around us—of course it cannot be always fresh, any more than the freshness of dawn or of springtime can last. Neither material nor mental states can retain their exquisite and subtle charm, and spiritual states are no better off; "frames and feelings" have an inherent tendency to subside into flatness, dulness, staleness, or whatever else expresses the want of freshness. There is only one unfailing source of unfailing freshness—Christ Himself. "Thou hast the dew of Thy youth"—the only dew that never dries up through any heat or dust. "Christ in you, the hope of glory." His word is, "For her." Your word should be, "Thou, O Lord, art my glory." I know it seems a great thing to claim, but the indwelling of Christ is not something reserved for only a few very exalted saints. The words are very plain: "Know ye not your own selves, how that Jesus Christ is in you, except ye be reprobates?" Take it just as you see it there. Jesus Christ is in you, if you have opened the door of your heart to let Him come in. He is "in you the hope of glory," if you have admitted Him; and He *is* your glory. If so, you may sing, "My glory *is* fresh in me,"

and never fear a change to Job's minor! He
had but a prophetic glimpse, through shadowing
centuries, of a Redeemer yet to come; you
have the full view of the fact of His finished
work, and His promised, and therefore present,
presence all the days; so this mournful experience only proves how different yours is
meant to be.

Jesus Christ is *always* fresh.

Don't we know it? Do we not always find
Him so, when we are in direct personal com-
munication with Him, with "nothing between"?
Are we not conscious that when we lament over
want of freshness, it really means want of Jesus?
We go and bemoan about it to a friend perhaps,
and ask what to do; and all the while, down
at the bottom, we are secretly aware that they
can do nothing more or better than advise us to
"go and tell Jesus"—to get into direct personal
contact with Him, alone with Him, again! The
very same time we spent, in this sort of second-
hand cistern-seeking, would be far more resultful
if spent in re-opening communion with Him,
and drawing from the Fountain itself. That is
always open. "All my fresh springs are in
Thee," not in our kind Christian friends.

All that we receive from Jesus is *always* fresh.

How fresh His most familiar words come, when He gives them to us by His Spirit! What is ever fresher than the old, old story, when any part of it is heard with the ear of faith? and our response is, "Jesus died for *me!*" What is ever fresher, whether in outward sacramental act, or in the thousand times repeated heart communion which waits not for time and place, than the remembrance of the exceeding great love of our Master and only Saviour, with its appropriating echo, "Jesus loves *me!*" The water that we draw out of these wells of salvation is always fresh indeed. And so is the manna on which He would have us feed continually.

And so is the oil with which He anoints us. There is the great first anointing to be His kings and priests, wherewith He "*hath* anointed us" (2 Cor. i. 21). Then comes the present, "Thou anointest my head with oil," as His received and honored guests, sinners though we be, when the table is prepared, and the cup runneth over, and we realize our new position as partakers of His grace. But then comes, "I *shall be* anointed with *fresh* oil!" A beautiful Future for all the days of our life; the always fresh anointings, the continual "supply of the

Spirit of Jesus Christ." Fresh oil of joy in the midst of the mourning through which we may pass, fresh oil of gladness in fellowship with our holy King (Ps. xlv. 7), fresh oil of consecration as day by day is given up to Him who has redeemed our lives, fresh oil upon the sacrifice as we offer our "praise to God continually, that is, the fruit of our lips."

Fresh springs, fresh oil, fresh glory!

With such resources, ought we to feel dusty? Is not the fault in ourselves? And if so, what is to hinder us from coming at once to the Triune source of all blessed renewal and freshness? It is Jesus our Saviour who is the ever fresh glory within us. It is the Holy Spirit, our Comforter, who shall pour His fresh oil upon us. With such resources, ought we not to refresh those around us? Ought they not to take knowledge of us that we have such a well of water within us, springing up into everlasting life? Ought there not to be a dewy fragrance in our lives, in our words and ways, that may silently witness to the reality of the source of our freshness? It is one of our special privileges to do this.

IX.

This God is our God.

"This God is our God."—PSALM xlviii. 14.

WHEN once we have obeyed the beseeching command, "Be ye reconciled to
God," and, being justified by faith, have peace
with God through our Lord Jesus Christ, we
have a right as His reconciled children to take
the strong consolation of these words. They
are then a seal of appropriation upon the whole
revelation.

Every part of God's word is a revelation,
more or less clear, of Himself. When we do
not see this, it is only that we miss it, not that
it is not there. Do we not know how very
possible it is to read the historical parts merely
as history, and the prophetical merely as prophecy, and the doctrinal merely as doctrine, and
miss the vision of God which everywhere shines
through the glass darkly, if only His good Spirit
opens our eyes to see it! And even when we do
trace out God Himself in His recorded works
and ways, how often we miss the personal com-

fort of remembering our own close and personal
interest in what we see of His character and
attributes.   It makes all the difference to recollect, at every glimpse of these, that *"this* God is
our God ! "

It is wonderful what a freshness and reality
the simple application of this little verse will
give to all our reading.   Just try it at once, whatever may be the next passage you read !   I
question if there is a single chapter, from the
first of Genesis to the twenty-second of Revelation, which will not reflect the light of this
beautiful little lamp.   First ask for the direct
and present and fresh anointing of the Holy
Spirit, that you may behold your God.   And
then, whether your gaze is turned upon a promise which reveals Him as the Loving One, or a
warning which reveals Him as the Just and Holy
One; whether you read a history which shows
His grand grasp in ordering the centuries, or a
verse which shows His delicate touch upon the
turn of a moment—as you admire, say, "*This*
God is our God."   When you read "Great
things doeth He which we cannot comprehend,"
and the splendid variety of His book gives a
glimpse of His power and glory in upholding
the things which are seen, from the hosts of

million-aged stars to the fleeting flakes of the
"treasures of the snow," say, "*This* God is our
God."

When you come to the many direct and
gracious declarations of what God is, you will
find these words light them up splendidly.
"The Lord, the Lord God, gracious and merciful, longsuffering, and abundant in goodness and
truth." *This* God is our God! "The Lord
is good, a stronghold in the day of trouble."
This God is our God! "Glorious in holiness,
fearful in praises, doing wonders." *This* God
is our God! "God is love." *This* God is our
God!

When you come to those parts of the Bible
which are too often undervalued and left out of
the daily reading, still, though it may be through
a less transparent veil, God will reveal Himself.
For instance, when you come to the genealogies
in Chronicles, consider how His individual care
is illustrated by the otherwise unknown names,
noted in His book because of their connection
with Christ; no matter how remote that connection, through the distant generations and
collateral branches, might seem to human ways
of thinking. And then remember that "this
God," who thus inscribed their individual names

for Christ's sake, is "our God" who has inscribed our individual names in the book of life
for Christ's sake, because we are chosen in Him.
And when we read the life of His dear Son, and
see what that beloved Son, in the infinite love-
ableness of His exquisite perfection, must have
been to the Father who yet spared Him not;
and, most of all, when we read of the hand of
God being laid upon the Man of His right
hand, when He made the iniquities of us all
to meet on Him, and let Him suffer unto
death for us men and for our salvation, then,
above all, let us turn to God the Father and
say, "This God, who *so* loved the world, is
our God!"

It seems as if this personal relationship to us
as our "God," were one in which He specially
delights, and which He would have us keep
continually in mind. In Deuteronomy, that
wonderful book of remindings, He has caused
this gracious name, "the Lord thy God," or
"the Lord your God," to be written no less
than two hundred and twenty-seven times. What
a name for Him to be revealed by to the way-
ward wanderers of Israel! and what comfort to
us that He is the same God to us! When you
want a helpful Bible subject to work out, sup-

pose you take this, and trace out all through the Bible under what circumstances or with what context of precious teaching He gives these words, and let the gladness of the search be "This God is *our* God." And then trace out (with your concordance if you like,) the responses to this constantly repeated and heart-strengthening Name, noting and arranging the passages that speak of "Our God." Between these you will find every soul-need for time and eternity supplied, from the first great need of the awakened sinner who is met with the words "He that is our God is the God of salvation," to the fulness of present blessing, "God, even our own God, shall bless us," and the fulness of future joy when "thy God (shall be) thy glory."

As you study, the claim will grow closer, and the response will intensify from the wide chorus of "Our God" to the fervent thrill of the whisper, "O God, Thou art *my* God."

Some of us may have an unexpressed notion that, after all, this does not come so near to us as the thought of "Jesus, my Saviour." We almost feel dazzled at the vastness of the idea of "God." And we take refuge, mentally, in what seems more within reach. This is almost always the case in the earlier stages of our Christian life. Having been drawn by the Father to the Lord Jesus Christ, we almost lose sight of the Father in the Son, instead of beholding the glory of God in the face of Jesus Christ as He intends us to do. Practically, some of us know consciously only one Person in the Blessed Trinity, and do not honor the Father as we honor the Son. If so, let us ask the Holy Spirit to lead us on into all truth, and to mature our spiritual powers and widen our spiritual vision that we may know more of what God means when He reveals Himself, not only by some name which human relationships enable us to grasp, but as our *God.*

We shall not love Jesus less, but more, as we learn to love God, who was in Christ reconciling us to Himself. We shall not be less tenderly grateful for His coming to die for us, but more, as we rise to adore the mystery of love which alone illumines the inconceivable eternity of the past when the Word was with God and the Word was God.

We shall find, too, that, while there is more than scope enough in the thought and revelation of God *as* God for the strongest hour, the very zenith of our intellect, there is rest in it for the weariest hour of the weakest frame. For when my heart and my flesh faileth, God is the strength of my heart and my portion for ever. And this God *is* our God for ever and ever. He will be our guide *even unto death.*

For the sad and sinful
  Shall His grace abound;
For the faint and feeble
  Perfect strength be found.
I, the Lord, am with thee,
  Be thou not afraid!
I will help and strengthen,
  Be thou not dismayed!
Yea, I will uphold thee
  With My own Right Hand,
Thou art called and chosen
  In My sight to stand.

X.

Thy Hand.

"Thy hand presseth me sore."—PSALM xxxviii. 2.

WHEN the pressure is sorest, the hand must be nearest. What should we do in suffering if we were left to imagine that it was Satan's hand that presses so sore! Our Father has not left us in any doubt about it. This settles it: "Thy hand"; "Thou didst it" (Ps. xxxix. 9); "It is the blow of Thine hand" (Ps. xxxix. 10); "Thy hand was heavy upon me" (Ps. xxxii. 4). It cannot be otherwise, for "in the shadow of His hand hath He hid you" (Isa. xlix. 2); and how can any other press you there? What is hid in God's hand must be out of reach of Satan's.

The hand is the most sensitive member, gifted with the most quick and delicate nerves of touch. When it presses, it instinctively measures the pressure; the contact is the closest possible; the throb which cannot be seen is felt, truly and immediately. This is how His dear hand is pressing you; this is what the pain means.

Have you ever watched the exceedingly delicate and yet firm pressure of the hand of a
skilful tuner? He will make the string produce
a perfectly true note, vibrating in absolute ac-
cord with his own never changing tuning-fork.
The practised hand is at one with the accurate
ear, and the pressure is brought to bear with
most delicate adjustment to the resistance: the
tension is never exceeded, he never breaks a
string; but he patiently strikes the note again
and again, till the tone is true and his ear is
satisfied, and then the muscles relax and the
pressure ceases. The string may be a poor little
thin one, yielding a very small note; but that
does not matter at all; it is wanted in its place:
just as much as a great bass one, that can yield
a volume of deep sound. The tuner takes just
the same pains with it, and is just as satisfied
when it vibrates true to the pitch, retaining its
own individual tone. That string could not
tune itself, and no machine was ever invented
to accomplish it; nothing but the firm and
sensitive pressure of the tuner's own living hand
can bring it into tune.

Will you not trust your Tuner, and begin a
note of praise even under the pressure?

"Yet take Thy way; for sure Thy way is best,
Stretch or contract me, Thy poor debtor.
This is but tuning of my breast,
To make the music better."—GEORGE HERBERT.

I take this pain, Lord Jesus,
As Thine own gift,
And *true* though tremulous praises
I now uplift;
.I am too weak to sing them,
But Thou dost hear
The whisper from the pillow—
Thou art so near!

'Tis Thy dear hand, O Saviour,
That presseth sore,
The hand that bears the nail-prints
For evermore.
And now beneath its shadow,
Hidden by Thee,
The *pressure* only tells me
Thou lovest me!

XI.

"I pray for them."—JOHN xvii. 9.

HE ever liveth to make intercession for us; and so while you have been silent to Him, He has been praying for you. If His hand has been upon you so that you could not pray, why need you be mourning over this, when your merciful and faithful High Priest has been offering up the pure and sweet and costly incense of His own intercession? But if your heart condemns you, and you know you gave way to indolent coldness when you might have roused yourself to more prayer, will it not touch you to recollect that, in His wonderful long-suffering, Jesus has been praying instead!

What confident and powerful petitions for His disciples he was pouring out when He said, "I pray for them." And how gracious of Him to let us overhear such breathings of Almighty love on their behalf. If He had said no more than this, we might have tremulously inferred that, being always the same Lord, He might give us a remote share of some reflected

blessing from this prayer.   But He anticipates
a wish that we should hardly have been bold
enough to form, and says: "Neither pray I for
these alone, but for them also which shall believe on Him through their word."   Have you
believed on Him through their word?   Then
you have His plain and positive assurance that
He was praying for you then, that verse by verse
you may take that prayer of prayers and say,
"Jesus prayed this for *me*."   And now that He
is the centre of the praises of heaven, whence
no other echo floats down to us, what is our
one permitted glimpse of the continual attitude
and occupation of this same Jesus?   "Who is
even at the right hand of God, who also maketh
intercession for us."   That is what He is doing
for you *now*.

> Praying for His children
>   In that blessèd place,
> Calling them to glory,
>   Sending them his grace;
> His bright home preparing,
>   Faithful ones, for you;
> Jesus ever liveth,
>   Ever loveth too.

MARCHING ORDERS.

[*These "Marching Orders" were written by request, for the "Church Missionary Gleaner." The slight variations were made by F. R. H., when she copied and sent them to the Editor of the Woman's Foreign Missionary Society, in Philadelphia, March,* 1879.—*M. V. G. H.*]

"Tell it out among the Heathen."

[*Ps. xciv.* 10, *P. B. V.*]

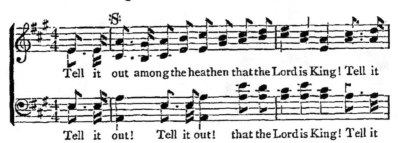

Tell it out among the heathen that the Lord is King! Tell it

Tell it out! Tell it out! that the Lord is King! Tell it

out! Tell it out! Tell it out among the nations, bid them

Tell it out!

out! . . . . Tell it out! Tell it out! Tell it out! bid them

Tell it out! Tell it out with a- do -

shout and sing! Tell it out! Tell it out! Tell it out!

FINE.

Tell it out! Tell it out! Tell it out with a- do -

shout and sing! Tell it out! Tell . . . it out! Tell it out!

64

-ra-tion that He shall increase; That the

that He shall increase; That the
-ra-tion that He shall increase; That the mighty King of Glory is the

that He shall increase; That the

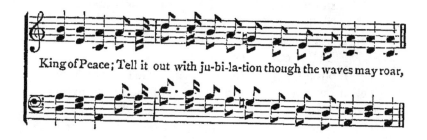

King of Peace; Tell it out with ju-bi-la-tion though the waves may roar,

That He sit-teth on the waterfloods, our King for evermore. Tell it

2.

Tell it out among the heathen that the Saviour reigns !

Tell it out ! Tell it out !

Tell it out among the nations, bid them burst their chains !

Tell it out ! Tell it out !

Tell it out among the weeping ones that Jesus lives;
Tell it out among the weary ones what rest He gives:
Tell it out among the sinners that He came to save;
Tell it out among the dying that He triumphed o'er
  the grave.

3.

Tell it out among the heathen Jesus reigns above!
        Tell it out!   Tell it out!
Tell it out among the nations that His reign is love!
        Tell it out!   Tell it out!
Tell it out among the highways and the lanes at home:
Tell it out across the mountains and the ocean foam!
Like the sound of many waters let our glad shout be,
Till it echo and re-echo from the islands of the sea!

Frances Ridley Havergal, 1872.

NO. I

"Go ye therefore, and teach all nations."—MATT.
xxviii. 19.

"Go" does not mean "send." "Go" does
not mean "pray." "Go" means "*Go!*" simply
and literally.

Suppose the disciples had been content to
take this command as most of us take it!
Suppose three or four of them had formed a
committee; and the rest had said, "You see if
you cannot find a few suitable men to train and
send to Rome, and Libya, and Parthia; and we
will see what we can do about collecting funds,
and anyhow subscribing a penny a week or a
pound a year ourselves!" How would the good
tidings of great joy and the glorious news of the
resurrection have spread at that rate? But they
did not subscribe—they went! Happily they
had not silver and gold to give, so they gave
themselves to their Lord and to His great work.
Jesus had said, "I have given them Thy word";
and very soon "great was the company (margin,

army) of those that published it," and grand
were the results.

The company of those that publish the word
of our God is very small in proportion to the
numbers that are perishing for lack of knowledge.   We are so accustomed to hear of the
millions of India and China, or of the immense
distances of America, that we get hardened to
them.   We do not take it in, that one man is
standing alone among perhaps a hundred thousand dying souls; or placed alone in a district
of a thousand square miles with forest and rapid,
and days of travelling, between every station in
that district.   Even from one of the best provided centres of missionary work in India a
friend writes that every missionary she has seen,
whether clerical, lay, or lady worker, has work
enough of his or her own to divide *immediately*
among at least six more, if they would only
come.   Yet our Lord's very last command was
" Go ! "

The company is still smaller in proportion to
those who might go if they only had the heart
to go.   Setting aside those who have not sought
or found Christ for themselves, and who do not
care to hear or read about these things, and
those to whom the Lord has definitely closed

this door by unmistakeable circumstantial guidance, there must be, as a mere matter of figures, thousands of young Christians who might go or put themselves in training for going. Yes, *thousands*, who have "freely received" salvation for themselves, but are not ready to "freely give" themselves to their Saviour's own great work; not ready even to take the matter into consideration; not ready even to *think* of turning aside out of their chosen profession or comfortable home course. Yet the command, the last that ever fell from His gracious lips before He went up from the scene of His suffering for us, still rings on, and it is "*Go!*" And He said, "if ye love Me, keep My commandments."

NO II.

"Go *ye*, therefore."—MATT. xxviii. 19.

WHEN we read any general promise, faith appropriates it by saying "This is for *me!*" And then it becomes effectual; one receives it as surely as if it had been spoken to and for one's self alone. When we heard the word of the Lord Jesus saying, "Come unto Me, all *ye!*" we who believe on Him did not and do not hesitate to say, "That means me!" and to act upon the gracious invitation.   Now is it fair to accept His "*Come* ye," and refuse His "*Go* ye"?   Is the first, with its untold blessings, to be appropriated personally, notwithstanding its plural form, and the second to be merely read as an interesting general command to whomsoever it may concern, but certainly not to ourselves?

As we have the unspeakable privilege and comfort of knowing that "all God's promises are for all God's children," so that you and I may claim every one unless we can show cause that it *cannot* apply to our case, so it must be that all God's commands are for all God's children, unless we can show cause that any one *cannot* apply to our case.   Therefore it follows that, as the Lord Jesus Christ said "Go ye," the obligation lies upon each of His true followers to consider definitely, at least once in his or her life, whether the circumstances in which He has placed them do or do not definitely preclude them from literally obeying this distinct and most literal commandment.

If they are really thus precluded, the loving and loyal heart will be eager to find ways of obeying the spirit of it.   But if *not* thus precluded, what then? To Him, your own Master, you must give account why you do not go! To Him you must "make excuse." To Him who gave Himself for you, and who knows exactly how much it is in your heart to "keep back" from Him. To Him who knows your secret preference for some other profession, or your reluctance to be tied to an absorbing life work; and who knows how you satisfy your conscience with offering Him the chips and shavings of your time and strength, a few odds and ends of work in the evenings or on Sundays, or a proportion of your time subtracted from "social claims," when you *might*, nobly, bravely, loyally, leave all and follow Him, responding to the Master's "Go ye," with "Here am I, send *me!*"

Have you thought of it in this light? If not, do not risk being among His disobedient servants, but take the matter direct to Himself, and say, "Lord, what wilt Thou have *me* to do? Make Thy way straight before my face!"

NO. III.

"And Jesus came and spake unto them, saying, All power is given unto Me in heaven and in earth. Go ye therefore."—MATT. xxviii. 18, 19.

THE Father is the source of all power. For "Thine, O Jehovah, is the greatness and the power." The Holy Spirit is the Communicator of power, so that those who bring their emptiness to be filled with the Spirit may say: "Truly, I am full of power by the Spirit of the Lord." But our Lord Jesus Christ is the Depositary of the power. As in Him are hid all the treasures of wisdom and knowledge, so in Him is "the hiding of His power" who has delivered all things unto the Son of His love.

All power is given unto Him, our Saviour, our Master, absolutely, unlimitedly, eternally! It is such a happy thought. As love and knowledge gradually supplanted fear, how delighted, one might almost say how proud, the disciples must have been, as miracle after miracle revealed the power of Jesus of Nazareth. Yet they did not know that He had *all* power. *We* know it, for He has told us. Do not our hearts respond "Worthy is the Lamb that was slain, to receive power!" "Let us be glad and rejoice, and give honor to Him!"

All power is given unto Him. First, power
to give eternal life to as many as His Father
has given Him; then power on earth to forgive sins; then power to uphold all things.
And these really include all power in heaven
and in earth. *All* power. For there is no
other power at all. "There is no power but of
God." All else that seems power is but the
impotent weakness, the unavailing spite, of a
vanquished foe. How quietly He disposes of
it when He says, not to veteran apostles, but to
His mere recruits: "Behold, I give unto you
power . . . . . . over all the power of the
enemy!" What must the reserve be when this
small delegated share is to overmatch "*all* the
power of the enemy!"

All power is given unto *Him.* Not to us,
for we could neither receive it nor use it. But
to Him for us. For "all things are for your
sakes." Joined to Him by faith we change our
weakness into strength, for His power flows into
us, and rests upon us. It is not that our weakness
is made a little stronger, but that His strength
is made perfect in our weakness. The power
of the Head energizes the feeblest member.

But our Master makes no barren statements
of unresultful positions. "All power is given

unto Me." What then? "Go ye *therefore.*" Who will take Him at His word, and, relying upon Jesus as our great Depositary of power, say, "*I will go in the strength of the Lord*"?

NO. IV.

"Freely ye have received, freely give."—MATT. x. 8.

THE context shows that we must not content ourselves with applying this only to silver and gold. Those to whom the command was spoken neither possessed nor provided any. Far greater gifts had they received, far greater gifts were they to give.

What have we freely received! Our Bibles give us a threefold answer. 1. Love: God our Father says, "I will love them freely." 2. Justification: for we are "justified freely by His grace," and "by His blood." 3. Life: for He says, "I will give unto him that is athirst of the fountain of the water of life freely." And unto us has been preached this "gospel of God freely."

We are responsible not only for having received such gifts, but for knowing that we have received them, for "we have received . . .

the Spirit which is of God, that we might know
the things that are freely given to us of God."
The whole Bible is one long inventory of the
things that are freely given to us, and yet we
cannot reckon our wealth, for "*all* things are
yours." Possessing the one unspeakable gift,
Jesus Christ Himself, is "possessing all things."

"As every man hath received the gift, even so
minister the same." How will you do this? Can
you make it a question of shillings or pounds,
dollars or cents? Is *that* what you have received?
Is that *as* you have received? Will you not say,
"I will freely sacrifice unto Thee"? Sacrifice!
what? "I beseech you therefore, brethren, by
the mercies of God, that ye present your bodies
a living sacrifice." Is there not one reader of
the *Church Missionary Gleanor* and of *Woman's
Work*, who, having "received Christ Jesus the
Lord," will go at His word, and "freely"
make known the good news of life from the
dead, and healing and cleansing through Him?
There are so many who would delight to
go, but whose way God has entirely hedged
up. Are there none whose way is not so
hedged up? He who spared not His own
Son, but with Him freely gives us all things, is
saying, very clearly and loudly, "Whom shall I

send, and who will go for us?" Will any one who *might* say, "Here am I, send me!" refuse to say it?

NO. V.

"*Therefore* said He unto them, The harvest truly is great, but the laborers are few: pray ye *therefore* the Lord of the harvest that He would send forth laborers into His harvest."—LUKE x. 2.

LOOK at these two "therefores." The first gives the reason for one of our Master's sayings; the second for one of His commands.

1. The Lord Jesus sent out the seventy: not to go where they liked; not to take their chance of lighting on the right place or persons. Not to begin His work where it might or might not be followed up. But He sent them before His face into every city and place *whither He Himself would come.* Unto Him should the gathering of the people be, and the coming presence of the Lord of the harvest proved that a harvest was waiting for the reapers. "*Therefore* said He unto them, The harvest truly is great, but the laborers are few." Is it not encouraging to think that He, in whose ways is

continuance (Isa. lxiv. 5), works in the same
way now, and sends us, whether at home or
abroad, into the places whither He, Himself, is
coming? Whether an English or American Sun-
day School, or an Indian city, if the Master Himself sends His servant or His handmaid into it,
it is because He, Himself, will come thither,
blessing His reapers and receiving His sheaves.
What an honor to be one of the "few" fore-
runners of the King, the herald of a silent yet
real and mighty advent of the Very God of Very
God !

II. Because the harvest is great and the laborers few, the Lord Jesus said, "Pray ye *therefore* the Lord of the harvest that He would
send forth laborers into His harvest." If the
fact remains, the command remains. And the
fact does indeed remain. And we have no
excuse in not knowing it. We, the readers of
the *Church Missionary Gleaner* and of *Woman's
Work*, know how great the harvest is, and we
know how few the laborers are. We cannot
say, "Behold, we knew it not." The need is
recognized, and the Lord has put the supply
within reach of the voice of prayer and the hand
of faith. He has told us what to do, and so now
the responsibility rests upon us.

Perhaps we read these pages and we sorrow a little for the burden of the King of princes, and wish the accounts were more glowing. But we do not turn the passing emotion into obedient and faithful and purposeful prayer, and so our sluggard soul desireth and hath nothing. "*He* shall not fail nor be discouraged"; but if we fail as His "helpers" in this easiest and most graciously appointed share of His glorious work, how shall we hope to share in our Master's harvest joy, and what claim shall we have to join in the great harvest Hallelujah?

NO. VI.

"Pray ye therefore the Lord of the harvest, that He would send forth laborers into His harvest."—LUKE x. 2.

MOST likely we never went to a missionary meeting in our lives but what we were told to pray for the work. We are quite used to it, we take it as a matter of course, and as the right and proper thing to be said. Nobody disputes for an instant that it is a Christian duty. But—*are we doing it ?*

As it is an acknowledged obligation upon all

who profess to love the Lord Jesus Christ that
they should obey His commandments, it is clearly a real obligation upon us, upon you and me,
to obey *this* commandment. And if we are not
doing it, we are equally clearly directly disobey-
ing our dear Master, and failing in the one test
of personal love to Himself which He gave us in
the same night in which He was betrayed.

Yes, *are we doing it?* Did you pray this morning what He bade you pray? Did you yesterday? Or last week? Surely it is no light thing
to go on from day to day leaving undone a
thing which we ought to have done, and about
which His own lips gave the most explicit direction!

How often we have sorrowfully felt that "we
know not what we should pray for as we ought!"
Now here is something that we *know* we are
to pray for. We know that it is according to
His will, or He would not have bidden us ask
it. And "if we ask anything according to His
will, He heareth us." And if we know that He
hears us in whatsoever we ask, we know that we
have the petitions that we desired of Him. See
what a splendid conclusion we reach! Oh,
"pray ye therefore!" And if we thus pray,
like little children, exactly what Jesus bids us

pray, see if we do not find a real and probably
conscious and immediate blessing in the very act
—the floodgates opened, the spirit of grace and
of supplication poured out, and the parched
tongue filled with prayer and praise !

It is an immense help to be systematic in
prayer. Many are finding it useful to take one
of the seven petitions of the Lord's prayer as
the keynote of their own each morning. This
brings "Thy kingdom come" to Monday morning. What if all the readers of the *Church Missionary Gleaner* and of *Woman's Work* should
accept this as a continual reminder, and at least
that *once* in each week join in fervent pleading
of this Christ-taught petition, including in it the
special one that the Lord would send forth laborers ! Let us agree as touching this that we
shall ask, in the obedience of faith and in the
name of Jesus.

NO. VII.

"Prayer also shall be made for Him continually."—
PSALM lxxii. 15.

VERY reverently, yet rejoicingly, let us accept
these words exactly as they are written. Most
likely we have read them with private revision

of our own, and supposed them only to mean, "Prayer also shall be made *unto* Him continually." But see! there it is, "*For* Him"!

To many it may be a new thought, to some a very startling one, that we are not only to pray to our King, but *for* our King. Yet words cannot be plainer, and we lose untold sweetness by gratuitously altering them.

For whom shall prayer be made? There can be no doubt as to this. The glowing, far-reaching statements and promises of this most Messianic psalm could never apply to any mortal monarch. Solomon in all his glory is but the transparent typical veil through which we discern the far excelling glory of Messiah and "the glorious majesty of His kingdom." And the only word which for a moment seems to dim the clearness is this one, "*For* Him." But gaze once more, and let Love arise and come to the aid of Faith, and her quick eye shall pierce the shadow and trace new splendor through it. The more fervently we love any one, the more we want to pray for them. The very thought of the loved one is changed into prayer when it glows under the pressure of spirit.

Intercession is the very safety valve of love. We all know or have known this. There is

solace and relief and delight in doing something
for the object of our love; but the more our
circumstances or ability or relative position
hamper us and make us feel that our acts can
bear but small proportion to our love (especially
when gratitude is a large element in it), the
more we feel that prayer is the truer and greater
outlet.   And when we have to feel that we
really can *do* nothing at all in return for some
remarkable kindness and affection, how exceedingly glad we are that we may and can *pray!*

Should there not be analogy here with the
"depth and height" of the love of Christ?   We
have talked unhesitatingly, sometimes even a
little boldly, of "working for Jesus."   And even
a glimpse of His "kindness and love" has been
enough to set us working "for Him," as we call
it.   Then comes a clearer and brighter view of
the "exceeding great love of our Master," and
we are pressed in spirit, and all the work we
ever could or can do for Him is seen to be just
nothing, and oh how we *do* want to do more
"for Jesus"!   Now has not our God provided
a beautiful safety valve for the full hearts of His
loving children in this most condescending
permission and command?   Not only "to Him
shall be given of the gold of Sheba," but "*prayer*

also shall be made *for Him*"! Yes, we may pour out our hearts in prayer for our King, besides spending our lives in working for Him. And I do not know that there is any purer and intenser joy than such prayer, pressed out by adoring love. There is no room for looking at self and difficulties and troubles and fears, when there is a gush of prayer summed up in "Father, glorify Thy Son!" We know that He hears this, and that we have the petitions that we desire of Him. And we go on, pleading His own great promises to the Son of His love, and rejoicing at the same time in their certainty; praying that Jesus may see of the travail of His soul and be satisfied, even in our own poor sinful hearts and lives, and in those for whom or over whom we are watching, and in myriads more; asking that the heathen may be given Him for His inheritance, and that all nations may call Him the Blessed One; and widening out to the grand prayer for Him with which the psalm closes, "And let the whole earth be filled with His glory! Amen, and amen." For this psalm is not only Messianic, but emphatically missionary, and so the prayer which is so graciously suggested and ordered in it is really the sum and culmination of all missionary intercession. And it is the spirit of it which ennobles and ought quite to transfigure all our missionary intercession. Let us keep the bright thought before us, that this is really, even if indirectly and unconsciously, making prayer "for Him"; and I would humbly say that if we take it up and so frame our petitions that they shall be directly and consciously "*for Him*," we shall hardly fail to find freshness of power and gladness in thus entering simply and literally this singularly bright vista of prayer which God has opened for us.

NO. VIII.

"Talk ye of all His wondrous works."—PSALM cv. 2.

I WONDER how many of us have observed this among our marching orders! And how many of us have been obeying it? Think of the last month, for instance, with its thirty days; on how many of those days did we talk of all His wondrous works? And if we did so at all, how much less did we talk about them than about other things!

Just consider what a power in the world *talking* is! Words dropped, caught up, repeated, then ventilated, combined, developed, set brains and pens to work; these again set the tongues to work; the talking spreads, becomes general, public opinion is formed and inflamed, and the results are engraven in the world's history. This is what talking can do when exercised about the affairs of "the kingdoms of the world and the glory of them." And we, who have been translated into the kingdom of God's dear Son,—we have tongues too, and what have we been talking about? How have we used this same far-spreading power? Only suppose that for every time each English-speaking Christian had talked about the day's news of the kingdoms of this world, he had spent the same breath in telling the last news of the kingdom of Jesus Christ to his friends and casual acquaintances! Why, how it would have outrun all the reports and magazines, and saved the expense of deputations, and set people wondering and inquiring, and stopped the prate of ignorant reviewers who "never heard of any converts in India," and gagged the mouths of the adversaries with hard facts, and removed missionary results and successes from the list of "things not generally known!"

God intends and commands us to do this.

We often quote "All Thy works shall praise Thee, O Lord, and Thy saints shall bless Thee." That sounds tolerably easy; but what next? "They shall speak of the glory of Thy kingdom, and talk of Thy power." Is this among the things that we ought to have done and have left undone? Are we not verily guilty as to this command? "Lord, have mercy upon us, and incline our hearts to keep *this* law!"

Perhaps we say we have kept it; we have had sweet converse with dear Christian friends about the Lord's kingdom and doings, and surely that is enough? No! Read further; there is not even a full stop after "talk of Thy power." It goes on to say why, and to whom; "To make known to the sons of men His mighty acts, and the glorious majesty of His kingdom." Not just talking it over among our like-minded friends, exchanging a little information maybe; but talking *with purpose*, talking so as to make known what great things our God is doing, not gently alluding, but *making* the sons of men *know* things that they did not know were being done. Some very intelligent and well educated "sons of men" do not seem to know that there is such a thing as "His kingdom" at all; and whose fault is that? They do

not and will not read about it, but they could
not help the "true report" of it reaching their
ears if every one of us simply obeyed orders
and *talked*, right and left, "of the glory of Thy
kingdom," instead of using our tongues to tell
what we have just seen in the newspapers.

But the bottom of not talking is generally the
not having much to talk about. When our
Lord said, "Out of the abundance of the heart
the mouth speaketh," He knew what was in
man better than we know ourselves. We don't
give ourselves the trouble to fill our hearts so
that they cannot help overflowing. If we gave
even the same time to supplying our minds with
the telling, yes and thrilling facts, happening
day by day in His kingdom, that we give to the
"other things" reported in papers and periodi-
cals, we should quite naturally talk of all His
wondrous works. We should *want* to tell people
what we had read and heard, not stale news
picked up accidentally months ago, but something interesting from its very freshness in our
own minds. When we have just read of a remarkable political event, or military victory, don't we
forthwith *talk* about it? And if the next person
we meet has not heard of it, do we hesitate to
tell him all we know about it on the spot? It

does not look as if we cared very much about our glorious Captain when we are not sufficiently interested in His latest victories in the mission field even to talk about them, *especially* to those who know nothing at all about them.

Now! what can we find, even in this month's magazine, which we can tell and talk about to those who have not read it? Begin at once!

NO. IX.

"The Captain of their salvation."—HEBREWS ii. 10.

Who gives the marching orders? Ah! that is the secret of their force, that is the secret of the thrill with which they have reached the hearts of men and women who have hazarded their lives to carry them out, faithful unto death, in their noble, literal obedience. For it was the voice of the Captain of their salvation that they recognised and followed, as the "Go ye therefore" fell upon their opened ears.

Of *their* salvation only? Is He not also the Captain of *our* salvation? Has not the Father given Him to be a Leader and Commander, and exalted Him to be a Prince and a Saviour for *us*? And shall His marching orders be disregarded, whatever they are, by one whose salvation He brought with His own arm, whose life He bought with His own blood?

For think how His Divine captaincy was won! No lightly or easily assumed leadership was that. A solemn and mysterious qualification of unknown sorrows and agonies was necessary. "For it became Him, for whom are all things, and by whom are all things, in bringing many sons unto glory, to make the Captain of their salvation, perfect through sufferings." Through wounding for our transgressions, through bruising for our iniquities, through chastisement and stripes, "through death," yes, "the *suffering* of death," did our Lord Jesus Christ pass to be made our perfect Captain, so that no soldier of His should ever have to endure any hardness or any fight of afflictions, without that real, personal sympathy from his Master which can only be the outflow of real, personal experience of the same. Oh, think of "the things that He suffered," over and above the great atoning suffering on the cross, just that He might personally know our little sorrows, and personally enter into our insignificant sufferings, and succor us in them with His own mighty help! "For in that He Himself hath suffered, being tempted,

He is able to succor them that are tempted."
Think of all that detail of suffering through His
lonely life and lonelier death being just the detail
of *love*,—love freshly marvellous in this aspect.

And now that the suffering is over, and the
Captaincy is won, and we are enrolled to be
His faithful soldiers and servants unto our lives'
end, is it to be merely a nominal thing on our
side? It was no nominal thing on His side.
The sufferings of the Lord Jesus were not
nominal, and His exaltation to be a Prince as
well as a Saviour is not nominal; then shall we
dare to treat His orders as merely nominal, and
as something to be comfortably explained away,
according to circumstances? Oh, if our loyalty
were as literal as His love, if our obedience were
as literal as His sufferings, would there, could
there be such want of volunteers to go where
He has plainly set up His standard, and such
want of free-handed pouring into His treasury,
and such want of brave speaking out of heart-
abundance, and such want of fervent, faithful,
persevering echoes of the great prayer, "Father,
glorify Thy Son!"

But if, by His grace, we are seeking honestly
to obey His marching orders, we shall find that
the very effort of obedience will quicken our

faith and love; the more we listen the more real and familiar will the voice of our Captain become, and the closer we follow the clearer will be our realization of His Leadership. And then we shall take up the exultant words: "Behold, God Himself is with us for our Captain!" and know the full blessedness of being ranged under the victorious banner of Immanuel.

Fierce may be the conflict,
　Strong may be the foe, ·
But the King's own army
　None can overthrow.
Round His standard ranging
　Victory is secure,
For His truth unchanging
　Makes the triumph sure.

Joyfully enlisting,   We are on the Lord's side,
　By Thy grace Divine,   Saviour, we are Thine.

Chosen to be soldiers
　In an alien land,
"Chosen, called, and faithful"
　For our Captain's band,
In the service royal,
　Let us not grow cold;
Let us be right loyal,
　Noble, true, and bold.

Master, Thou wilt keep us,   Always on the Lord's side,
　By Thy grace Divine,   Saviour, always Thine!

(92)

"Say amongst the heathen, that the Lord reigneth."
Ps. xcvi. 10.

SUCCOTH. 87, 87, 77.

1 HERALDS of the Lord of glcry!
    Lift your voices, lift them high:
  Tell the gospel's wondrous story,
    Tell it fully, faithfully;
  Tell the heathen midst their woe
  Jesus reigns, above, below.

2 Haste the day, the bright, the glorious!
    When the sad and sin-bound slave
  High shall laud, in pealing chorus,
    Him who reigns, and reigns to save.
  Tempter, tremble! Idols, fall!
  Jesus reigns, the Lord of all!

3 Christians! send to joyless regions
    Heralds of the gladdening word;
  Let them, voiced like trumpet legions,
    Preach the kingdom of the Lord;
  Tell the heathen, Jesus died!
  Reigns He now, though crucified.

4 Saviour, let Thy quickening Spirit
    Touch each herald lip with fire;
  Nations then shall own Thy merit,
    Heart shall glow with Thy desire:
  Earth in jubilee shall sing,
  Jesus reigns, the eternal King!
            Rev. William Henry Havergal, 1827.

(No. 881, "Songs of Grace and Glory.")

THE seven following subjects are copied from F. R. H.'s outlines of the addresses given in her parlor, November and December, 1878. The illustrations which enriched them, the sacred songs or solos aptly introduced, the stirring appeals, the beseeching voice, passed unrecorded. But they are not forgotten; hence the testimony of her village hearers: "Miss Frances *still* speaks to us; her voice follows us, especially the words, 'Be ye holy for I am holy'; and 'without holiness no man shall see the Lord.' She was God's mouth to us."

EXTRACTS FROM LETTERS TOUCHING THESE MEETINGS.

To S. G. Prout.

Nov. 6th, 1878. . . . "Now I want you to do me a good turn. I want you to find a minute to spare, when you are bringing other needs before your Master, to ask for me a real great blessing on an open Bible class which I am starting this evening. I don't know who will come, few or many, but I want real converting grace poured out, and I want to be enabled so to speak of Jesus that they may be won to Him. There is the centre. How it just goes through one, when one touches upon His own beloved name! And how we do want Him to be understood and loved!"

To J. K.

Nov. 7th. . . . "I don't know how to thank you enough for your prayers. I made a delightful start last night with about thirty. I think there is a fair prospect next time of filling every available space and chair. I started at once on the *Christian Progress* lines (giving each the explanatory paper, and re-questing all to read the chapters every day). The very first result showed I was justified, for that same evening our dear little Christian maid got leave (indeed I think they asked her) to read the evening portion in the kitchen. Mr. and Mrs. Tucker and many others seem taken with the idea of joining me and the other fifteen thousand readers. I can't think why other workers don't see the value of this Union, as I do. What *can* you do better for those whom you have won, or are trying to win, than thus to ensure them two good meals a day! I am most thankful that I was distinctly led to start at once with the *C. P.* Union.

"F. R. H."

LEPROSY. (*Nov. 6th*, 1878.)

LEVITICUS XIII.

Symptoms. Various outwardly. But always:

(1) Deeper than the skin (ver. 3; Isa. i. 5, 6).

(2) Spreading (ver. 7). Compare white hair (Hos. vii. 9.)

(3) Infectious.

Effects of leprosy:

(1) Isolation (ver. 45).

(2) Exclusion from the camp (ver. 46; Rev. xxi. 27).

(3) No cure but by the direct hand of God (Num. xii. 10, 13).

(4) Progressing unto death. ("Grew worse," Mark v. 26; 2 Tim. ii. 13; Matt. xii. 45.)

1. Not some, but all, have sin (Rom. iii. 23).

2. Feeling makes no difference; sin is a *fact* (Ps. li. 5).

3. In leprosy the priest first looked (Ps. cxix. 132; Heb. iv. 13; John ii. 25), then pronounced the leper unclean (John v. 22).

4. Priests could neither cure nor cleanse; Jesus does both. Compare Hos. v. 13 and vi. 1. Compare Matt. viii. 3, Exod. xv. 26.

5. *How* Jesus heals. "He was wounded for

our transgressions, He was bruised for our iniquities, the chastisement of our peace was upon Him, and with His stripes we are healed" (Isa. liii. 5).

A devoted minister going to dwell in the leper island of Molokai, voluntarily leaving his home and his country, exposing himself to contagion, disease, and death, out of love to the souls of the poor outcast lepers dwelling there, is the nearest illustration. Still he could not take the leprosy *instead* of the lepers. But the Lord Jesus was "made sin for us, who knew no sin, that we might be made the righteousness of God in Him" (2 Cor. v. 21). Took sin *upon* Him, *off* us.

6. Only one case in which the leper was pronounced clean (Lev. xiii. 12, 13), if *all* covered. So "only acknowledge" (1 John i. 9; Isa. lxiv. 6; Rom. vii. 18), and turned white (Isa. i. 18; Ps. li. 7).

7. Christ always healed leprosy without *delay* or *means* (Matt. viii. 3. Contrast Matt. xv. 23 and John ix. 7). "The Same" now, immediate cleansing in His blood.

8. Nothing to hinder except not coming. "Ye will not come to Me, that ye might have life" (John v. 40).

9. Claim this by faith. Healing *only* in God's way (Acts iii. 16, iv. 12, xiv. 9). Say, "Heal me, O Lord, and I shall be healed" (Jer. xvii. 14).

10. Then praise! "And one of them, when he saw that he was healed, turned back, and with a loud voice glorified God" (Luke xvii. 15). "O Lord my God, I cried unto Thee, and Thou hast healed me" (Ps. xxx. 2, ciii. 2, 3).

11. *Continual* healing and *continual* cleansing. "The blood of Jesus Christ His Son cleans*eth* us from all sin" (1 John i. 7).

HOLINESS, AND BEING GOD'S OWN.

(*Nov.* 13*th*, 1878).

'And ye shall be holy unto Me: for I have severed you from other people, that ye should be Mine."—LEV. xx. 26.

I. WHAT God would have us be—holy unto Himself. *First step* to holiness is seeing our sinfulness (Lev. xiii. 12, 13; Isa. vi. 5).

1. *Need* of holiness. "Holiness, without which no man shall see the Lord" (Heb. xii. 14, 21, 27).

2. *Command.* "Be ye holy, for I am the

Lord your God" (Lev. xx. 7). "But as He which hath called you is holy, so be ye holy in all manner of conversation; because it is written, Be ye holy for I am holy" (1 Pet. i. 15, 16).

3. *Enabling grace* in Himself. "I am the Lord which sanctify you" (Lev. xxi. 8). Sevenfold (Phil. ii. 12, 13).

4. *Promise and purpose.* "For whom He did foreknow He also did predestinate to be conformed to the image of His Son" (Rom. viii. 29). "For this is the will of God, even your sanctification" (1 Thess. iv. 3). "Whom the Lord doth choose, he shall be holy" (Num. xvi. 5).

II. Three reasons for holiness.

1. Because He is holy. "Who is like Thee, glorious in holiness!" (Exod. xv. 11.) "Holy, holy, holy, is the Lord of hosts" (Isa. vi. 3). Effect on Isaiah, ver. 5.

God the Father holy: "Holy Father" (John xvii. 11). God the Son: "Thine Holy One" (Acts ii. 27). God the Spirit: "the Spirit of holiness" (Rom. i. 4). Trinity: "Holy, holy, holy, Lord God Almighty, which was, and is, and is to come" (Rev. iv. 8).

Holiness is the dividing line between saints and sinners (Ps. xcvii. 10–12; Rev. xv. 4).

Wonderful that this *holy* God loves us and wants us to be holy, and will make us "partakers of His holiness" (Heb. xii. 10).

2. Because God has separated His people unto Himself. Israel a type of believer's separation (1 Cor. x. 11, τύποι).

(1) Command. "Wherefore come out from among them, and be ye separate, saith the Lord" (2 Cor. vi. 17).

(2) Promise. "And I will receive you, and will be a father unto you, and ye shall be My sons and daughters, saith the Lord Almighty" (2 Cor. vi. 17, 18). "Seemeth it but a small thing unto you, that the God of Israel hath separated you from the congregation of Israel, to bring you near unto Himself?" (Num. xvi. 9.) "But know that the Lord hath set apart him that is godly for Himself" (Ps. iv. 3). Illustration: The brave, the loyal, the soldiers of unswerving allegiance and obedience, are chosen for the royal body guard, "The Queen's Own!"

3. Because He wants us to be His *own*. "*Mine.*"

(*a*) To be His people (Heb. viii. 1c). I am your God (Lev. xx. 8).

(*b*) Servants (John xx. 10; Ps. cxvi. 16). Master (John xiii. 13).

(*c*) Children (Jer. iii. 4).   Father (Jer. iii. 19).

(*d*) Bride (Hos. iii. 3).   Husband (Hos. ii. 19, 20; Isa. liv. 5).

(*e*) Peculiar treasure (Ps. cxxxv. 4).   Exceeding great reward (Gen. xv. 1).

(1.) To His "own."   Don't only say, " *We* are Thine" (Isa. lxiii. 19), but "*I* am Thine" (Ps. cxix. 94).   He replies: "Fear not, for I have redeemed thee, I have called thee by thy name; thou art Mine (Isa. xliii. 1).   "*For*" price indeed (1 Cor. vi. 19, 20; 1 Pet. i. 18, 19; 2 Sam. vii. 21-24).   Evidence given (Mal. iii. 16, 17).   Have you not a word for Jesus? (Mal. i. 6.)

(2) But *are* you His own?   Illustration: Forlornness of a child not belonging to anybody. Do you "belong to Christ"?   If not, you belong to a secret owner whose slave you are (Rom. vi. 16).   But

"Come to be Thine, yea Thine alone."

(Of the touching tenderness of F. R. H.'s appeal no record can be given.)

CHRIST OUR LAW-FULFILLER. (*Nov. 20th,* 1878.)

"These are the commandments which the Lord commanded Moses for the children of Israel in Mount Sinai."—LEV. xxvii. 34.

These commands, what we have read in Exodus and Leviticus. Two great divisions, the ceremonial law and the moral law. Christ the *end* of both (Rom. x. 4.).

I. Ceremonial law. Burdensome and costly. Contrast, "My yoke is easy and My burden is light" (Matt. xi. 30).

All performed through priests. "And every priest standeth daily, ministering and offering oftentime the same sacrifices, which can never take away sins: but this Man, after He had offered one sacrifice for sins for ever, sat down on the right hand of God. For by one offering He hath perfected for ever them that are sanctified" (Heb. x. 11, 12, 14).

All this only "a shadow of good things to come"; "a shadow of heavenly things" (Heb. x. 1, viii. 5). Describe the shadow, and contrast it with the substance. Christ the substance. *He* is a continual object lesson, teaching of Himself and His offices and of our need of

atonement. Heb. ix. 9, 10: "until." Christ
the end of all this.

II. Moral law.   This law was

1. *Reflection of God's holiness;* forbidding
all contrary, enjoying all accordant.   Witness
to the law is placed within us — conscience,
answering only if awake.   Illustration: If a
witness is drugged he can give no evidence,
no response.   Sin drugs the conscience (Rom.
vii. 11–16).

2. *The moral law is summed up in two great
commandments* (Matt. xxii. 37–40).   These are
put in one word by St. Paul, love!   "Love
is the fulfilling of the law" (Rom. xiii. 10).

3. The moral law is *not done away with.*
"Verily I say unto you, Till heaven and earth
pass, one jot or one tittle shall in no wise pass
from the law till all be fulfilled" (Matt. v. 18).
Some confuse between the ceremonial and the
moral law.   Christ not only did *not* destroy the
moral law, but gave it a fuller meaning and a
wider reach, applying all to the heart as well as
our outward observance (Matt. v. 21–45).   "Sin
is the transgression of the law" (1 John iii. 4).
"The soul that sinneth it shall die" (Ezek.
xviii. 4).   The Commandments are read in our
Communion Service, and the prayer after each

is, "Lord, have mercy upon us, and incline our hearts to keep this law." It would be well if this was done in chapels also.

4. If the moral law is not done away with, it *has got to be fulfilled.* Mark the word: not *one* thing done that ought not to be, not *one* left undone. *Not* doing harm is *not* fulfilling the law; you will never get to heaven by what you have *not* done. It would be no excuse for a servant who had broken a china vase to say, "I have not broken the window *and* the china." "For whosoever shall keep the whole law, and yet offend in *one* point, is guilty of all" (James ii. 10). This is not my saying but God's; and Christ says, "The word that I have spoken, the same shall judge him in the last day" (John xii. 48). Illustration: If only *one* link was broken in the chain let down to pull you out of the shaft of a mine, the danger is the same, even if every other link were unbroken.

Tests: "Search the Scriptures" (John v. 39); and, "Thou shalt love the Lord thy God with all thy heart, and with all thy soul, and with all thy mind" (Matt. xxii. 37). Even if all else kept, have you *searched* the Scriptures, have you loved God with all your heart?

Therefore, "all have sinned and come short

of the glory of God" (Rom. iii. 23).   Illustration: Describe the ice crevasses in the pass of St. Théodule; travellers roped to the guide; if that rope breaks once only, danger.   Besides, God says, "Neither shall they cover themselves with their works" (Isa. lix. 6).

5. Christ is the end of *this* law *for* righteousness *to* every one that believeth.

The very first thing He said He came to do. "Think not that I am come to destroy the law or the prophets: I am not come to destroy, but to fulfill" (Matt. v. 17).   God said, "He will magnify the law and make it honorable" (Isa. xliii. 21).   Christ said: "Lo, I come: in the volume of the book it is written of Me.   I delight to do Thy will, O My God: yea, Thy law is within My heart" (Ps. xl. 7, 8).   *Why* did Jesus Christ live thirty-three years?   *Why* not simply come down to die?   It was to do for us just what we have *not* done and could not do, "fulfill all righteousness."   This had got to be done by some one for us; that is, instead of us.   "For as by one man's disobedience many were made sinners, so by the obedience of one shall many be made righteous" (Rom. v. 19). "Many be made righteous," but *who* are they. All them that believe, "for the righteousness of

God which is by faith of Jesus Christ is unto all
and upon all them that believe" (Rom. iii. 22).
So Jesus is our "righteousness" (1 Cor. i. 30).
"And this is His name whereby He shall be
called, THE LORD OUR RIGHTEOUS-
NESS" (Jer. xxiii. 6).   Then we may say, "All
our righteousnesses are as filthy rags" (Isa. lxiv.
6); and, "I will greatly rejoice in the Lord, my
soul shall be joyful in my God, for He hath
clothed me with the garments of salvation, He
hath covered me with the robe of righteousness" (Isa. lxi. 10).

6. *Therefore* let us keep the commandments.
Jesus said, "If ye love Me, keep my commandments" (John xiv. 15).   "For the love of Christ
constraineth us" (2 Cor. v. 14).   Love evidenced by obedience, "He that hath My commandments, and keepeth them, he it is that
loveth Me" (John xiv. 21); and faith evidenced
by works, "Even so, faith if it hath not works
is dead" (James ii. 17).   What about seeking
for *all* the commandments of the Lord?   This
is a further step; He wants us to "seek for
all the commandments of the Lord your God"
(1 Chron. xxviii. 8).   He wants us to keep
"*all* . . . always."   "Oh that there were
such an heart in them, that they would fear

Me, and keep *all* My commandments always"
(Deut. v. 29). Because, "the Lord commanded
us to do all these statutes, to fear the Lord our
God for our good always" (Deut. vi. 24). And
God promises in the new covenant, "I will
put My laws into their mind, and will write
them in their hearts" (Heb. viii. 10). Pray,
"Make me to go in the path of Thy commandments" (Ps. cxix. 35); and "Write all
these Thy laws in our hearts we beseech Thee."
It is very humbling when the Holy Spirit's light
flashes upon some command of our God which
we have never observed, and of course have never
kept. Do ask that blessed Spirit to show you
not only your sin in not keeping His commands,
but also the remedy, the precious blood of Christ.
Come to that Fountain, and you will find the
cleansing, sanctifying, and overcoming power of
the blood of the Lamb.

In conclusion, what are *you* going to do about:
1st, believing; and 2nd, obeying? John xiv.
21, 23: "He that hath My commandments
and keepeth them, he it is that loveth Me."
"If a man love Me, he will keep My words."
"Moreover by them is Thy servant warned,
and in keeping of them there is great reward"
(Ps. xix. 11).

THE VOICE FROM THE MERCY SEAT.
(*Nov. 27th.* 1878.)

"And when Moses was gone into the tabernacle of the congregation to speak with Him, then he heard the voice of One speaking unto him from off the mercy seat that was upon the ark of testimony, from between the two cherubims: and He spake unto him."—NUM. vii. 89.

WHAT has this to do with us? Everything—for God "hath in these last days spoken unto us by His Son" (Heb. i. 2).

I. The Ark. II. The Mercy Seat. III. The Voice from it.

I. The Ark. See Exodus xxv. 10–16. "When we find Christ in the law, that law becomes gospel."

A.—1. The ark was of shittim wood and gold, typifying the human and Divine nature of the Lord Jesus.

2. "Overlaid with gold," not two parts separable, but all the wood overlaid with gold; hence Christ was "perfect God and perfect man."

3. Crown of gold round about the mercy seat; type of "royalty," and the "throne of grace."

4. Rings and staves for carrying the ark; the gospel to be preached to all nations.

5. In the holy of holies it was dark; contrast in heaven, the holiest of all, no created light needed.

B.—1. What was the ark for? To contain the tables of God's law. Refer to our last lesson; Christ our law-fulfiller: "Thy law is within my heart" (Ps. xl. 8).

2. The ark was described and ordered and provided (1) *before the law was written* (Exod. xxxi. 18, and xxxii. 15, 16); so Christ was foretold and provided before; never a moment when Christ was not: (2) *before the law was broken,* God foresaw; so before He gave the law which He knew would be broken He provided a Mediator and Substitute to keep it perfectly.

3. The ark contained the *second* set of tables; first broken, never pierced together again (Exod. xxxii. 19), renewed set (Exod. xxxiv. 1, 4, 28). Adam broke the Divine law, therefore the first covenant at an end. So have we broken the law, therefore no covenant of works avails. If one party breaks conditions, a contract is null. Therefore God renewed and placed it in better hands; put it into an ark which held it safe till all it required was fully accomplished.

II. The mercy seat.

1. Gold only. Mercy God's prerogative (Mark ii. 7).

2. Exact size. "And thou shalt make a mercy seat of pure gold; two cubits and a half shall be the length thereof, and two cubits and a half the breadth thereof" (Exod. xxv. 17). As *wide* as Christ's whole nature; *no wider*, because no mercy *out* of Christ. See Heb. x. 28, 29, and 2 Cor. v. 19.

3. Kept in place by the crown. Sovereignty and kingly righteousness. "A God all mercy were a God unjust."

4. The mercy seat covered the tables of the law. "God shut up its curses and hushed its thunders." Now, it is not the law that speaks condemnation, but the blood of Jesus speaks acquittal from the mercy seat.

> "Thine was the sentence and the condemnation,
>   Mine the acquittal and the full salvation."

5. The mercy seat, place of God's especial presence and glory and meeting place (Ps. lxxx. 1; Exod. xxv. 22). "There will I meet with thee," in *Christ.* Promise and fulfilment.

III. The voice from the mercy seat.

1. It was when Moses went to the appointed

place that he heard the voice. We shall not hear God's voice of mercy unless we come to Christ. Jesus said unto him, I am the Way, the Truth, and the Life, no man cometh unto the Father but by Me" (John xiv. 6). "Wherefore He is able also to save them to the uttermost that come unto God by Him" (Heb. vii. 25).

2. Moses heard it from the mercy seat. Contrast Gen. iii. 8; Ps. lxxxv. 8; Acts x. 36.

3. Voice speaking "unto *him*"; so it is individual.

4. Spoke for direction and guidance.

Application. What do we know of God speaking to us from the mercy seat? He speaks through Jesus. "Jesus speaks and speaks to thee," etc. He says, "I have somewhat to say unto thee" (Luke vii. 40), and "I have yet many things to say unto you" (John xvi. 12). Are we saying, "Master, say on," and "Speak, Lord, for Thy servant heareth"? And Jesus said, "The words which I speak unto you, they are spirit and they are life" (John vi. 63). Don't we want these "words"? and reply, "I will watch to see what He will say unto me" (Hab. ii. 1). Illustration: the Queen's dinner party. Surely every voice would be hushed to hear her speak. Do we ever listen for the "still small voice"? He says, "I will speak comfortably unto her" (Hos. ii. 14; Isa. l. 4). Let our response be, "I will hear what God the Lord will speak" (Ps. lxxxv. 8), and "Say unto my soul, I am thy salvation" (Ps. xxxv. 3).

He appoints the meeting place, all the day long He is stretching forth His hands to us. He *is* speaking, are we neglecting to hear His voice? "How shall we escape if we neglect so great salvation, which at the first began to be spoken by the Lord?" (Heb. ii. 3). "He that rejecteth Me and receiveth not My words hath One that judgeth him: the word that I have spoken, the same shall judge him in the last day" (John xii. 48, 49).

He still "waits." "Come *now* and let us reason together, saith the Lord, though your sins be as scarlet they shall be as white as snow, though they be red like crimson they shall be as wool" (Isa. i. 18).

Think *who* it is that waits. Jesus the Son of God. "For we have not an high priest which cannot be touched with the feeling of our infirmities, but was in all points tempted like as we are, yet without sin. Let us *therefore* come boldly unto the throne of grace, that we may obtain mercy, and find grace to help in time of need" (Heb. iv. 15, 16). Having therefore, brethren, boldness to enter into the holiest by the blood of Jesus, by a new and living way which He hath consecrated for us through the veil, that is to say, His flesh; and having an High Priest over the house of God; let us draw near with a true heart and in full assurance of faith" (Heb. x. 19–22).

FORGIVENESS. (*Dec. 4th,* 1878.)

"Pardon, I beseech Thee, the iniquity of this people according unto the greatness of Thy mercy, and as Thou hast forgiven this people from Egypt, even until now."— NUM. xiv. 19.

NEWS of forgiveness is only interesting to those who are conscious of sin.

I. Who pleaded. II. Who forgave. III. Who was forgiven. IV. Extent of forgiveness.

I. Who pleaded: Moses.

(1) *Mediator.* "Moses His chosen stood before Him in the breach to turn away His wrath, lest He should destroy them" (Ps. cvi.

23). So Christ: "for there is one God and one Mediator between God and men, the man Christ Jesus" (1 Tim. ii. 5).

(2) *Intercessor.* Had not shared the sin. So Christ, "who needeth not daily, as those high priests, to offer up sacrifice, first for his own sins and then for the people" (Heb vii. 27). "It is Christ that died, yea, rather that is *risen* again, who is even at the right hand of God, who also maketh intercession for us" (Rom. viii. 34). Moses never pleaded in vain except for himself. "And the Lord said, I have pardoned according to thy word" (Num. xiv. 20). So Christ, "and I know that Thou hearest Me always" (John xi. 42).

II. Who forgave? *Thou.* "Forgiving iniquity and transgression and sin" (Exod. xxxiv. 7). "Who can forgive sins but God only?" (Mark ii. 7.)

III. Who was forgiven! "This people," described as "a disobedient and gainsaying people" (Rom. x. 21). "A stubborn and rebellious generation, a generation that set not their heart aright, and whose spirit was not steadfast with their God." "How oft did they provoke Him in the wilderness and grieve Him in the desert" (Ps. lxvii. 8, 40).

IV. Extent of forgiveness. "From Egypt," all along, murmurings, rebellings, idolatry, stupidity, etc., "until now." Climax of their sin, "were it not better for us to return into Egypt!" "Let us make a captain and let us return into Egypt." "All the congregation bade stone them with stones" (ver. 3, 4, 10). Yet, "Thou *hast* forgiven this people"; "and the Lord said, I have pardoned according to thy word." (Then turning to the piano, F. R. H. sang

LOVING ALL ALONG.

TRAMP, tramp on the downward way,
With seldom a stop and never a stay,
Loving the darkness, hating light,
Our faces set towards eternal night!
Each has answered God's cry,
"Why will ye die? turn ye! turn ye!"
"Not I, not I!"
We have bartered away His gems and gold
For the empty husks and the shadows cold;
We have laugh'd at the Devil's tightening chains,
And bidden him forge them strong!
  And God has kept on loving us,
      Loving all along.

The love still flows as we tramp on;
A sorrowful fall in its pleading tone;
"Thou wilt tire in the dreary ways of sin;
I left My Home to bring thee in!

In its golden street stand no weary feet,
Its rest is glorious, its songs are sweet ! ''
    And we shout back angrily, hurrying on
    To a terrible home, where rest is none:
"We want not your city's gilded street,
Nor to hear its constant song ! ''
    And still God keeps on loving us,
       Loving all along.

And the tender Voice pursues each one:
" My Child, what more could thy God have done ?
Thy sin hid the light of heaven from Me,
When alone in the darkness I died for thee !
Thy sin of this day, In its shadows lay,
Between My face and One turned away ! ''
And we stop and turn for a moment's space,
Flinging back the love in the Saviour's face,
To give His heart yet another grief, and glory in the
      wrong !
    And Christ is always loving us,
       Loving all along.

One is bending low before the King,
And the angels listen with quivering wing;
He *has* entered the City and sings its hymn,
While the gold of its street through tears is dim !
" To Him who so loved me and washed me white,
To Him be all honor and power and might ! ''
That marvellous love no sin could move,
Waited, and wearied not, sought and strove !
To us, through the darkness, the Voice still calls
From the gleaming heights of the jasper walls;

To the long kept places our welcome waits,
      Amid the exultant throng.
  Chorus.—And God will still be loving us,
      Loving all along,
      And God will still be loving us,
      Loving all along!

Apply all this to our own case. Why do we
need forgiveness? Conscience tells, *if* enlight-
ened. Sins of deed, word, thought, commission,
omission, sins of this day, can you recollect?
yesterday? all the year? since childhood? (Ps.
xxv. 7.) We forget, but God recalls *all*, every
one either forgiven or unforgiven. Not *one*
who is unforgiven enters heaven; "and there
shall in no wise enter into it anything that
defileth, neither whatsoever worketh abomina-
tion or maketh a lie" (Rev. xxi. 27).

Then take the first and great command,
"Thou shalt love the Lord thy God with all
thy heart and with all thy soul and with all thy
mind"; are we not "guilty"? Then see Ps.
lxxvii. 22. "They believed not in God, and
trusted not in His salvation." Believed not!
trusted not! Guilty under *all* these counts, and
none the less for not seeing we are; sin itself
blinds us. Let each say now, "Father I have
sinned." What then? "There *is* forgiveness

with Thee, that Thou mayest be feared" (Ps. cxxx. 4, 7). "To the Lord our God belong mercies and forgivenesses, though we have rebelled against Thee" (Dan. ix. 9). That's much, but we want more. Then, "Thou Lord art good and ready to forgive" (Ps. lxxxvi. 5). God is "*ready*," but perhaps we are hardly "ready," and say, "I don't feel my sins enough" (you don't find that in the Bible); but God meets us with the promise that He will give us "*repentance* and *remission*" (Acts v. 31).

Perhaps it is the opposite with some of you, and you are saying, "My sins are *too* great to be forgiven." Then "Let the wicked forsake his way, and the unrighteous man his thoughts; and let him return unto the Lord, and He will have mercy upon him; and to our God, for He will abundantly pardon" (Isa. lv. 7, and i. 18; Ps. ciii. 3).

How can this be? "Through this Man is preached unto you the forgiveness of sins" (Acts xiii. 38).

How so? "If we confess our sins, He is faithful and just to forgive us our sins" (1 John i. 9). *Faithful* because He promised; *just* because Christ bore the punishment, purchased the forgiveness. Talk about "free" forgiveness; free to us, but cost Him blood. So "God for Christ's sake hath forgiven you" (Eph. iv. 32; 1 John ii. 12). What is bought *is* bought. So *in* Him "we have redemption through His blood, the forgiveness of sins" (Eph. i. 7; Ps. lxxxv. 2).

Will you believe the message to-night? "I have blotted out, as a thick cloud, thy transgressions, and as a cloud thy sins: return unto Me; for I have redeemed thee" (Isa. xliv. 22). (Illustration: There was once a deaf mute, named John. Though he never heard any other voice, he heard the voice of Jesus, knew it, loved it, and followed it. One day he told the lady who had taught him, partly on his fingers and partly by signs, that he had had a wonderful dream. God had shown him a great black book, and all his sins written in it, so many, so black! And God had shown him hell, all open and fiery, waiting for him because of all these sins. But Jesus Christ had come and put His *red hand*, red with the blood of His cross, all over the page, and the *dear* red hand had blotted all John's sins out; and when God held up the book to the light He could not see one left! (Isa. xliii. 25.)

Don't fear to take forgiveness at once. God

does not want long processes—He looks into the heart. If while sitting here any want to turn from sin and be forgiven, that is repenting; if any are saying, "Yes, I know it is all true of me," that is confession; and "If we confess our sins, He is faithful and just to forgive us our sins." Now take forgiveness, for "you, being dead in your sins and the uncircumcision of your flesh, hath He quickened together with Him, having forgiven you all trespasses" (Col. ii. 13). "When Jesus saw their faith, He said unto the sick of the palsy, Son, thy sins be forgiven thee" (Mark ii. 5). This same Jesus is here to-night.

What else? Shall sins come up again? In the new covenant God declares, "I will be merciful to their unrighteousness, and their sins and their iniquities will I remember no more" (Heb. viii. 12). Then Micah vii. 18, 19.

1. *Pardoneth.* (Illustration: "Ah, Willie," said a strong man in tears, "it's forgiven sin breaks a man's heart," etc.)

2. Will subdue.

3. Will cast all their sins into the depths of the sea.

"Blessed is he whose transgression is forgiven, whose sin is covered" (Ps. xxxii. 1).

THE BRAZEN SERPENT.   (*Dec.* 11*th*, 1878.)

"And the Lord said unto Moses, Make thee a fiery serpent, and set it upon a pole: and it shall come to pass, that every one that is bitten, when he looketh upon it, shall live.   And Moses made a serpent of brass, and put it upon a pole, and it came to pass, that if a serpent had bitten any man, when he beheld the serpent of brass, he lived."—Num. xxi. 8, 9.

No mistake about the application of the type, Christ Himself gives it: "And as Moses lifted up the serpent in the wilderness, even so must the Son of Man be lifted up: that whosoever believeth in Him should not perish, but have eternal life" (John iii. 14, 15).

I. What the sin was.

1. Discouragement (Ps. cvi. 24; lxxviii. 22).

2. Spake against God and against Moses.

3. Untruth: "no bread   .   .   .   no water."

4. Dissatisfaction with God's provision of manna.

All this was "tempting Christ" (1 Cor. x. 9).

II. The punishment.   "And the Lord sent fiery serpents among the people, and they bit the people; and much people of Israel died" (ver. 6).   The bite fatal, so the Devil's bite of sin.   Implied in the Hebrew word, "flying serpent" (Isa. xxx. 8).   Satan "goeth about," nothing out of his reach but what is in Christ's hand. "Fiery," beginning of the worm that never dies, the "everlasting burnings." Probably the bite induced fever and thirst.

III. The remedy. The serpent of brass, same form but no venom. "Christ made sin for us, who knew no sin" (2 Cor. v. 21). The *curse* (Gen. iii. 14; and Gal. iii. 13). Thus *doubly* Christ was made a curse for us.

"*Lifted up.*" So on Calvary, conspicuous, known, seen. So now: "And I, if I be lifted up from the earth, will draw all men unto Me" (John xii. 32); every time Christ is proclaimed.

"*Must be* lifted up" (ver. 14); compare Christ's "*musts*" for our sakes.

Remedy devised by God. "Yet doth He devise means" (2 Sam. xiv. 14); contrary to human reason or supposition.

No other remedy. Suppose an Israelite thinking the remedy too simple, too unlikely, trying some "first rate stuff," or going to the priest or physicians; all in vain, only *one* appointed way (Acts iv. 12).

All could see, so no excuse; all may look now.

Result of looking: life. "It shall come to pass"; "It came to pass."

Instant cure.   "When he looketh"—that moment—*now!*

Are you looking now? If so, "*saved.*" If
not, *unsaved*; the deadly bite working certain
death. Suppose an Israelite saying, "Yes, all
very true; but I'm tired to-night," or "going to
have my supper." If you found the serpent had
bit you, you would soon drop forks. (*e.g.*:
Describe a real scene at a supper table where
many were assembling after a mission service.
There were some still unsaved ones there, and
the sting of sin was so bitter that they could
not eat, could not conceal their distress; and
then and there we all knelt down, and then and
there they looked and lived. Then, with every
face bright, cured, and happy, how joyful that
supper time was.)

Must look for yourself; no one *can* look for
you. "Whom I shall see for myself, and mine
eyes shall behold, and not another" (Job xix.
27). In the last day no choice about looking
then, but too late for the saving look.

Command: "Look unto Me, and be ye saved,
all the ends of the earth: for I am God, and
there is none else" (Isa. xlv. 22). No option;
going on in disobedience as well as danger,
if you don't look.

Waiting till better: device of Satan.

No condition. "Whosoever," only *look*, "every one," "any man." "And this is the will of Him that sent Me, that every one which seeth the Son, and believeth on Him, may have ever-lasting life: and I will raise him up at the last day" (John vi. 40).

Must know you are bitten, or you won't look. Fancy an Israelite saying, "Don't see that I'm so very poorly; not *quite* right perhaps, but not like *that* poor fellow dying there," etc., etc.

Cure never failed. Ver. 19: "*Any* man . . . he *lived.*" "If *any* man . . . shall live for ever. . . . He that believeth on Me hath everlasting life" (John vi. 51, 47). Believe it! Israelite didn't need to feel his pulse, he *lived* and *knew* it. Take God at His word, and He will take you at yours.

Not only *not perish*, but *live, have* everlasting life. What does that imply? Everlasting salvation, joy, light, love, and with Him (1 Thess. v. 10). "Father, I will that they also whom Thou hast given Me be with Me where I am, that they may behold My glory" (John xvii. 24). Contrast the word *perish* and life. God knows what that word "perish" means. Jesus knows, and therefore *pleads* with you. The Devil knows, and hushes up the meaning. You don't know yet, but it's a terrible certainty.

What will it be to be lost for want of a look! Devil taunting through all eternity. "You *might have been* saved if you would have looked, and you wouldn't." And you risk *this* if you don't look to-night.

You who have looked:

1. *Tell others;* fancy an Israelite cured, and quietly watching others dying, without a word.

2. *Keep on looking.* "Looking unto Jesus, the author and finisher of our faith" (Heb. xii. 2). Many a little *snap* after the great bite is cured, but looking is both prevention *and* cure. "But mine eyes are unto Thee, O God" (Ps. cxli. 8). "Unto Thee lift I up mine eyes" (Ps. cxxi. 1).

3. *The "look"* now, the long blessed gaze then. "Thine eyes shall see the King in His beauty" (Isa. xxxiii. 17).

> "Is it for me to see Thee
>   In all Thy glorious grace,
> And gaze with endless rapture
>   On Thy belovèd face?"

THE CONTINUAL BURNT OFFERING.

(Dec. 18th, 1878.)

"And thou shalt say unto them, This is the offering made by fire which ye shall offer unto the Lord; two lambs of the first year without spot day by day, for a continual burnt offering. The one Lamb shalt thou offer in the morning, and the other lamb shalt thou offer at even. And a tenth part of an ephah of flour for a meat offering, mingled with the fourth part of an hin of beaten oil. It is a continual burnt offering, which was ordained in Mount Sinai for a sweet savor, a sacrifice made by fire unto the Lord."—Num. xxviii. 3–6.

Each of the offerings had a *special* teaching.

I. The circumstances of this offering, typifying Christ.

1. *God calls it "My* offering"; compare "God will provide Himself a lamb" (Gen. xxii. 8).

2. Two *lambs.* (1) Clean. (2) Valuable, (3) Good for food. (4) Harmless. (5) Meek. (6) Isa. liii. 6, 7; "*we* like sheep," therefore Christ the *Lamb.*

3. *Without spot* (1 Pet. i. 18, 19; 2 Cor. v. 21; 1 John iii. 5).

4. *Offering* made by fire. All circumstances of the *burnt* offering indicated suffering and wrath (Lev. i. 5–9). Killed, blood shed, flayed, cut into pieces, all burnt. So Christ suffered for sins (1 Pet. iii. 18), "died for" (1 Cor. xv.

3), "gave Himself for" (Gal. i. 4). *Real* (Luke
xxii. 44; Isa. lviii. 5; Ps. xxii. 14–17, xxxii.
8). "By Thine agony and bloody sweat, by
Thy cross and passion"; took *all that.*

Why was fire needful in these sin offerings?
Shows the wrath descending on the victim instead
of the offerer. (Describe lightning conductor;
the flash, once descending on that, passes into
the earth, spent, never returns, never strikes
again).

5. *Offered at the door of the tabernacle* (Exod.
xxix. 42). The Israelite could not go in to
worship, could not reach the shewbread and the
candlestick, nor even approach the veil, without
passing by the altar of burnt offering.

So Christ's offering of Himself for us, His
atonement, is the *very beginning.* All past and
present worship, without it, is mockery and iniquity, prayers and hymns and all.

6. *Day by day.* This the special point of the
type, teaching that continual sin needed always
atonement. The sin goes on day by day (if you
get a glimpse of that you would not dare to lie
down to-night without an interest in the atonement); but *now* the sin offering is done away.
Why? Because the Messiah was cut off but not
for Himself. "*He shall cause the sacrifice and*

the oblation to cease" (Dan. ix. 27). The shadow passed when the substance came. Christ made it to cease when He died (Heb. x. 1, 11, 12).

One sacrifice for sins *for ever*. Done, finished. "I have finished the work which Thou gavest Me to do" (John xvii. 4). "It is finished" (John xix. 30). "Christ was *once* offered to bear the sins of many" (Heb. ix. 28). An Israelite could never come and *not* find the altar there.

Morning and evening sacrifice, possibly, showed atonement for age and youth.

7. *It was a sweet savor*. Would God let His Son suffer *in vain?* Fire goes out when the fuel is burnt; no more flame. Justice satisfied, God satisfied (Eph. v. 2). "Christ also hath loved us, and hath given Himself for us, an offering and a sacrifice to God of a sweet smelling savor," does not mean that God was pleased to see Jesus suffer, but the result of those sufferings (John x. 17). If God is *satisfied*, why not *you?*

II. What will you do about it?

1. Are you unconverted or anxious? See the Israelite laying his hand on the head of the sin offering, showing the transfer—accepting it as substitute. ("This is my act and deed.") When you own the sin, and own Christ's death as your

substitute, then "*it shall be accepted for him*"—
the sacrifice burnt up instead of the offerer.
Nothing to do, nothing else will do.   Security
is not your *feeling* satisfied, but God's *being*
satisfied.   (Isa. xlii. 21).   Then *now* "behold,"
etc. (John i. 29).   He still says, "Behold Me,
behold Me" (Isa. lxv. 1).

2. You who have accepted the offering *are*
accepted in the Beloved.   What *must* follow?
"Who His own self bare our sins in His own
body on the tree, that we, being dead to sins,
should live unto righteousness; by whose stripes
ye were healed" (1 Pet. ii. 24).   "Forasmuch
then as Christ hath suffered for us in the flesh,
arm yourselves likewise with the same mind:
for he that hath suffered in the flesh hath ceased
from sin, that he no longer should live the rest
of his time in the flesh to the lusts of men, but
to the will of God" (1 Pet. iv. 1, 2).   "And that
He died for all, that they which live should
not henceforth live unto themselves, but unto
Him which died for them and rose again" (2
Cor. v. 15).   Titus ii. 14: "That He might
redeem us from all iniquity," not only from
wrath.   See Hebrews x. 10: "Once for all,"
that you might be *sanctified.*

As the continual burnt offering showed always

the present atonement for sins that are past, so it shows the continual cleansing for the present. "The blood of Jesus Christ His Son cleans*eth* us from all sin" (1 John i. 7). Must not, dare not, continue in sin, etc. "What shall we say then? . . . How shall we, that are dead to sin, live any longer therein?" (Rom. vi. 1, 2.)

III. *Christ, as the Lamb, is an eternal type.* See Rev. vi. 16: "the wrath of the Lamb." Will it fall on *us?* No wrath of the Lamb, for those washed in the blood of the Lamb. "There is therefore now no condemnation to them which are in Christ Jesus, who walk not after the flesh but after the spirit" (Rom. viii. 1). We shall for ever have to do with the *Lamb* of God. "Worthy is the Lamb that was slain to receive power, and riches, and wisdom, and strength, and honor, and glory, and blessing. And every creature which is in heaven, and on the earth, and under the earth, and such as are in the sea, and all that are in them, heard I saying, Blessing, and honor, and glory, and power, be unto Him that sitteth upon the throne, and unto the Lamb for ever and ever" (Rev. v. 12, 13; vii. 9, 14, 17).

CANTICLES I. 1–8.

Ver. 1: "The song of songs, which is Solomon's."

Solomon a type of Christ. This "song of songs" is Christ's song, the song which He puts into the hearts and lips of His children. Contrast with the "vanity of vanities" in Ecclesiastes. This song is also a type of the "new song." Christ's children are His bride, even if ever so weak and unworthy.

Ver. 2: "Let Him kiss me with the kisses of His mouth."

Kiss the token of love. "Mouth"; this gives a clue to the meaning of "grace is poured into thy lips" (Ps. xlv. 2); and "the gracious words which proceeded out of His mouth" (Luke iv. 22). Applied to our own hearts He says, "I will speak comfortably (margin) to her heart" (Hos. ii. 14). Have we experience of this, His words coming sweetly to our hearts? If so, we have had the "kisses of His mouth." If not, "oh taste and see"; "incline your ear"; "watch to see what He will say" (Hab. ii. 1); and then say, "Master, say on."

"For Thy love is better than wine" (ver. 2).

"Wine" is the symbol of all *earthly* refreshment and joy. Jesus gives the new wine of His love, and says, "Drink, yea, drink abundantly, O beloved" (Cant. v. 1); "Yea, come, buy wine and milk" (Isa. lv. 1).

Ver. 3: "Because of the savor of Thy good ointments Thy name is as ointment poured forth."

Let us begin with the second clause, "Thy name." How sweet the name which is above every name, Jesus (Phil. ii. 9). "Ointment": "the house was filled with the odor of the ointment" (John xii. 3). Oriental odors surpassingly fragrant. Appeal to you who really love the Lord Jesus; does not His very name bring a *thrill*, a fragrance? Jesus! If His name is *in* our hearts, its fragrance should fill the house. Sometimes this is not till the box is *broken*; many tongues not loosed till dying. But why thus? Why not, if we have the ointment, pour it out now, and be *living* witnesses, not waiting to be *dying* witnesses, for Him. Let others take knowledge of you that you have been with Jesus (Acts iv. 13).

What is His name? "Wonderful, Counsellor, the mighty God, the everlasting Father, the Prince of Peace" (Isa. ix. 6).

"*Because* of"; because not merely ointments poured forth, but the unfailing supply within. O name of *infinite* sweetness! Ointments denote its manifold preciousness. Perhaps we first come to love Christ for what He has *done*, for the pouring forth of the ointment; but then we go on to love Him for what He *is*, to rejoice in the ever unfolding sweetnesses of His perfections (1 Pet. ii. 7).

"*Therefore* do the virgins love Thee." Because He is *what* He is, so full of infinite sweetness and beauty and love and grace (Zech. ix. 17). "Love Thee." Do *we?* How worthy Jesus is of our love, of our desire to love Him. If we can't yet say, "Lord, Thou knowest all things, Thou knowest that I love Thee" (John xxi. 17), can we say "the desire of our soul is to Thy name," and "to the remembrance of Thee" (Isa. xxvi. 8)? If so, be encouraged, for "He will fulfil the desire of them that fear Him" (Ps. cxlv. 19). The promise is to them that *fear*, not even love.

Ver. 4: "Draw me, we will run after Thee: the King hath brought me into His chambers: we will be glad and rejoice in Thee, we will remember Thy love more than wine: the upright love Thee."

"Draw me." The more we find our utter helplessness, the more we find His strength and sufficiency. His "drawing" always comes before our "coming"; our cry to Him only the echo of His still, small voice (John vi. 44). It is a great mistake to think this great truth a reason for despair—it is reason for hope and confidence. If we have any desire, He gave it, and that is His *drawing*. Now—don't check and stifle His drawing; yield—run.

"Drawing" is the token of everlasting love (Jer. xxxi. 3). We desire because He *draws;* He draws because He *loves.* But let us "run," "press," "strive." No sauntering (1 Cor. ix. 24). "We *will* run": resolution, will, energy. Perhaps we feel we have no will, no energy; see how we need *all* from Him. If we have it, He gave it; if we have it not, we can only get it from Himself. Sweet paradox, in such *running* there is *rest.*

"Draw *me, we* will run." We should not come alone, but when "drawn" seek to win others. "After Thee." The secret of true running the heavenly race after Jesus is following close in heart, keeping near, abiding in Him, and also following His steps (1 Pet. ii. 21). Our collect well expresses this, "daily endeavor ourselves to follow the blessed steps of His most holy life." It is not running after anything or any one else, but Jesus only—"after *Thee*."

"The King hath brought me into His chambers." What is this? His dwelling place, His pavilion, the secret of His tabernacle, the secret of His presence (Ps. xc. 1; xxvii. 5. xxxi. 20; xxv. 14). This is no dream, but a reality. There *is* a "secret of His presence," into which He brings His children. Not at first perhaps, but by degrees. "I have yet many things to say unto you, but ye cannot bear them now" (John xvi. 12).

We could not explain it to another, *what* it is to feel Jesus near, to feel that we *are* brought into His chambers, but it is real, and unutterably sweet. It is such shelter in trouble, and such added sweetness in joy. What treasures of happiness are ready for us if we will but come to Jesus! "We will rejoice," etc. We *shall* if He thus brings us (Ps. xlv. 15).

"We will remember." How often forget! Contrast Isa. xlix. 15. Fulness of theme. We may remember part and yet forget the rest, love resolving and redeeming—living and dying. Let us *try* to remember and say Isa. xxvi. 8. Remember also *experience* of love—treasure it up for dark days. Communion Service: "To the end that we should always remember the exceeding great love of our Master and only Saviour Jesus Christ"; and He meets us in remembrance (Isa. lxiv. 5).

"The upright love Thee." Illustrate. Would it be "upright" if one entered service, were living and receiving wages, etc., and yet *did* nothing? If we profess to serve Christ, it is not "upright" if we do nothing for Him. Secret of lack of love, we mourn over coldness, then up and *work* for Jesus.

Ver. 5: "Black, but comely." "Black" (Isa. lxiv. 6; Rom. iii. 23, vii. 18). Can't see this but with opened eyes; the more light, the more we *see* the darkness. First we only mark sins of act, then word, thought, motive, feeling, then the whole array of uncountable omissions, the good we *might* have done and did not; then we resolve and try and fail, and find the utter sinfulness of which all this is only the fruit. If we saw it *all at once* we should be overwhelmed.

"But comely!" How? (Ezek. xvi. 14.) "My comeliness which I had *put* upon thee."

Eph. v. 26, 27: church composed of individuals. "Tents and curtains." Explain simile. "And let the beauty of the Lord our God be upon us" (Ps. xc. 17). But how shall *we* have this beauty? "Even the righteousness of God," etc. (Rom. iii. 22.) Do you believe? Ask your own hearts *now*, "Dost thou believe on the Son of God?" Then it is upon you, even if never realized before; *you* are justified and clothed in His beauty. Do not think it matters not; you can stand in nothing else before God. (Matt. xxii. 11–13.)

Ver. 6: "Look not upon *me*," but "Behold, O God our shield, and look upon the face of Thine Anointed" (Ps. lxxxiv. 9). God seeing us in Christ our representative. "The sun" throwing light upon it. Is it so with us? Backsliding, yielding under the hot sun of temptation or persecution? Then plead this verse.

"My *mother's* children were angry with me," *i.e.* earth's "children of this world" angry. This should not discourage, because our *Father* and His children will not be angry.

"Made me keeper," *e.g.* Sunday-school teachers; apply and appeal to them; only in cultivating our *own* vineyard are we likely to keep others'. But not only to keepers of other vineyards this applies: "mine own vineyard" applies to *all*, each has a vineyard which should bring forth fruit unto God. (Hos. x. 1.)

Ver. 7: "Tell me, O Thou whom my soul loveth, where Thou feedest, where Thou makest Thy flock to rest at noon; for why should I be as one that turneth aside by the flocks of Thy companions?" Our "tell me" always the echo of His whisper, "I have somewhat to say unto thee."

"Oh Thou whom my soul loveth" comes *after* "we will remember." Love of longing, not yet of nearness. Proof of love is the desire of nearness. There are three desires here: 1st, "tell me *where*"; 2nd, food (Matt. v. 6); 3rd, rest. At noon heat, weariness. Mark, not rest at night. Some one told me, "we must look forward for rest," but *no*, rest *now*, "at *noon*." With most of you it is now morning, but quickly morning rises into noon, and sooner or later you will crave *rest*. (Ps. xxiii. 2.) (Job xxxv. 29.) (Isa. xxvi. 3, 12.) (Matt. xi. 28.) Only "Thou," no other can make. "Makest"—sometimes He makes us weary first (Job xvi. 7), that He may win us to rest.

"Why should I be," in the margin "is veiled." Idea here is threefold.

(1) The bride was veiled when in the presence of strangers, orientals only unveiling at home and in the presence of most intimate friends.

(2) Veil is the token of distance, restraint, separation; contrast this with Christian communion.

(3) Veil the token of dim vision, veils and dimness constantly go together. Contrast, when the veil shall be taken away (2 Cor. iii. 16–18). From the veiled to veilless vision.

"Flocks of Thy companions." Wonderful title ! See also John xv. 15.

Ver. 8: Gentle rebuke implied, why do we not know? The Holy Spirit is promised to show all things, to teach all things, to guide into all truth.

"O Thou fairest." Compare chap. ii. 10, 14, and iv. 1, 8; Eph. v. 27. "Go thy way forth by the footsteps of the flock."

Our church services are often undervalued, *they* are the footsteps of Christ's flock for centuries back. The Te Deum and Communion Service are glorious echoes of the church militant. Distinct blessing on Christian intercourse. (Mal. iii. 16; Luke xxiv. 14, 15.)

Memoirs often a help, tracing the footsteps of others.

One path trodden by *all* the flock, prayer; they "come boldly unto the throne of grace."

(*Unfinished.*)

EVERLASTING LOVE.

"I have loved you, saith the Lord."—MAL. i. 2.

THIS is only the old, old story; but it is written with the finger of God; graven with the diamond pen of His unchangeable truth on the rock of His everlasting purpose; traced in golden letters on records of the universe; printed in characters of living, shining, glowing light on hearts of believers; written by the Spirit of the living God, not with ink but blood, precious blood of Christ, blood shed on the cruel cross for us. Query, is it written on our hearts? If not, O blessed Saviour, write it *now;* write if it be but the first line of this glorious inscription on every heart *here* and *now.*

"I have loved you, saith the Lord. *Yet* ye say, Wherein hast Thou loved us?"

I. *"Herein."* (1) "Herein is love, not that we loved God, but that He loved us, and sent His Son to be the propitiation for our sins" (1 John iv. 10). Sovereign love. "The Lord did not set His love upon you, nor choose you, because ye were more in number than any people; for ye were the fewest of all people; but because the Lord loved you" (Deut. vii. 7, 8).

"*Not* that we loved God." Our heart echoes this "not." "His thoughts are not our thoughts." The natural heart says, "God can't love me, because I don't love Him."

(2) "In this was manifested the love of God toward us, because that God sent His only begotten Son into the world" (1 John iv. 9). Gift of God (John iii. 16). "Gave," unto death. Love of the Son answering. "Greater love hath no man than this, that a man lay down his life for his friends" (John xv. 13).

(3) In quickening: "But God, who is rich in mercy, for His great love wherewith He loved us, even when we were dead in sins, hath quickened us together with Christ" (Eph. ii. 4, 5). Do we think enough of this further proof of His love; we who are not "dead in trespasses and sins," but feel and live?

(4) In adopting: "Behold," etc. (1 John iii. 1): Are any here feeling they have no part in this; outside the home and Father's love? say now, "I will arise and go to my Father" (Luke xv. 18).

(5) Bearing and carrying (Isa. lxiii. 9). *Has* He not "borne"? *has* He not carried? Even if we can't feel (3) and (4), we must own *this*.

Query: "Wherein" has thus a fivefold

answer. Turn from His book to the book of our own lives, and count up the proofs of this love. Include "chastening" (Heb. xii. 6).

II. *How?* Double answer (John xvii. 23, and John xv. 9). "As" (subject for study).

Perfect, love εἰς τέλος (John xiii. 1).

Sacrificing love. Father (Rom. viii. 32), Son (John xv. 13); both combined in Rom. v. 8.

Everlasting love (Jer. xxxi. 3). This brings us to:

III. *When* He loved us. (1) Before the foundation of the world (compare John xvii. 23, 24, 26).

(2) When we were yet sinners (Rom. v. 8; compare Hos. iii. 1; Isa. xlviii. 8, 10). "I knew."

(3) Before we recognized it (1 John iv. 19; Ezek. xvi 8). "When," "then," "time of love."

(4) After backsliding (Hos. xiv. 4).

(5) In death as in life (Cant. viii. 7). "Cannot quench," not those things in Rom. viii. 35, climaxing in violent death. For, Isa. xliii. 2 and Deut. xxxiii. 27.

(6) Through eternity: "Everlasting life Thou givest, Everlasting love to see." All included in that wonderful εἰς τέλος (John xiii. 1)

IV. Results of this love.

(1) Believing. Love begets love, this is the condition of the manifestation of love.

(2) Outward mark, "For the love of Christ constraineth us" (2 Cor. v. 14, 15; John xiv. 21, 23; John xvi. 27).

(3) What if *resultless*? (Lam. i. 12.) Appeal and application [no notes recorded].

V. Great question, how may we know that everlasting love is ours? (compare John vi. 44 with Jer. xxxi. 3).

How we yearn over the title, "disciple whom Jesus loved"! It applies to us also: "O man greatly beloved." May we all be able to say, "We have known and believed the love which God hath to us."

EVERLASTING LIFE.

"For the wages of sin is death; but the gift of God is eternal life, through Jesus Christ our Lord."—ROM. vi. 23.

THIS is the most important of all subjects, concerns each one: "that ye may know that ye have eternal life; and that ye may believe on the name of the Son of God" (1 John v. 13).

I. *What* is the gift? To value it, we must

look at the contrast; eternal death. He hath
"set the one over against the other."

The Holy Spirit has used only *one* word in the
original for the duration of both (Matt. xxv. 46).
No use imagining an alternative; no annihil-
ation, etc., etc.; instinct as well as revelation
tells this. After all arguments of infidels (over-
turned again and again by voices which they
won't go to hear and books which they won't
read) there remains an awful *if* which none
can set aside. *If* they turn out to be wrong,
if the Bible be true, *then* "what remaineth?"
"blackness of darkness for ever," "where their
worm dieth not, and the fire is not quenched"
(Mark xi. 46). But there is no real "if": God
has revealed all this.

Now contrast: "gift of eternal life"; life
which no decay can touch, no death can
shadow; in which the grave will be only "par-
enthesis," not "period"; gift worthy of Giver.
Why eternal? because not mere prolongation
of *our* life, but Christ's own eternal life given *to*
us, as His mortal life was given *for* us. "Because I live, ye shall live also" (John xiv. 19).
(Col. iii. 3,) Can Christ, the Very Life, die?
Faith makes one with Him, and partakers of
His life (Luke x. 42).

Describe eternal life. 1st, negatively; no sin, sorrow, pain, death, etc.: 2nd, positively: life of perfect love, knowledge, holiness, bliss.

II. *Who* is the Giver? The Father, "the gift of God is eternal life" (Rom. vi. 23). The Son, "I give unto them eternal life" (John x. 28). The Holy Spirit, "the Spirit giveth life" (2 Cor. iii. 6). Gift of the triune Jehovah; "King eternal, immortal, invisible." Value of the gift enhanced by consideration of the Giver.

III. *Who* may have the gift? First, the thirsty ones (Isa. lv. 1; John vii. 37). But even if not hitherto among these, and cannot claim "Blessed are they which do hunger and thirst after righteousness" (Matt. v. 6), a wider offer still. Secondly, "*whosoever* will" (Rev. xxii. 17): you and I.

IV. *Why* we may have eternal life. (1) Because God has promised it *for us to* Christ (Tit. i. 2). "In hope of eternal life," which God, that cannot lie, promised before the world began. *He* holds the promise for us (illustration of promise made *to* parents *for* a child). (2) Because Jesus has taken our sin and its wages, *death,* upon Himself, in our stead.

V. *How* we may have eternal life. "Only believe." "Believe on the Lord Jesus Christ, and thou shalt be saved" (Acts xvi. 31). "Verily, verily, I say unto you, he that heareth My word, and believeth on Him that sent Me, hath everlasting life, and shall not come into condemnation; but is passed from death unto life" (John v. 24). What can hinder? only one thing; we can't receive a gift in a *full* hand: "Nothing in my hand I bring." It is offered on no other terms, can be had on *no* other, than as a "free gift." Gift too, not to friends but to *debtors* and *enemies* (Rom. v. 6, 7, 8). How debtors? Take one point only (Mark xii. 30): "Thou shalt love the Lord thy God with all thy heart, and with all thy soul, and with all thy mind, and with all thy strength; this is the first command," absolute debt: who can dare say we have rendered obedience to this one command. Verily "nothing to pay." What if we persist in clinging to false hopes and vain efforts! (Illustration. Five sailors were clinging to the broken mast of a sinking ship in Dublin Bay. A rope was thrown to them. At the trumpet signal "Now!" they were to loose their hold of the mast, and trust themselves to the rope. Four did so, and were hauled safe to shore. The fifth hesitated to let go, and was lost!)

VI. *When* we may have eternal life. This very day and hour. Now! "He that believeth on the Son hath everlasting life" (John iii. 36). "Verily, verily, I say unto you, he that believeth on Me hath everlasting life" (John vi. 47). No reason *in* delay: "If you tarry till you're better, you will never come at all. (Illustration. One summer's evening a traveller hired a boat on a wide and apparently safe river. He was warned not to go too far, not to *delay* in turning, at a signal of danger, where the current swept down the falls of Niagara. He knew there *was* danger; after amusing himself still floating down the stream, he fell asleep. Onward, downward, went the boat, past the signal post; the sleeper slept on. Passers by on the shore shouted, "Stop!" "stop!" The sleeper woke; too late to turn back, one cry of despair—and he was hurled to the depths beneath.)

But perhaps you have eternal life without knowing it. Listen to God's word: (1 John v. 11). Rest your soul on this, and make God a liar no longer, but believe the record that "God hath given to us eternal life, and this life is in His Son."

NOTES FOR A YOUNG WOMEN'S CHRISTIAN ASSOCIATION MEETING.

I HAVE sometimes wondered at the knowledge of the Holy Spirit implied in Psalm li. But we see every operation of the Holy Spirit mentioned before the time of David. In our February subject we saw the sevenfold operations of the Holy Spirit. For this month observe the grouping. But first glance at Psalm cxliii. 10: "leading" being a specialty with Israelites in the desert. The Prayer Book version is beautiful: "Let Thy loving Spirit lead me forth"; compare Rom. xv. 30. We do not dwell enough on the *real* and *personal* love of the Spirit. He is no abstract idea, but a *loving Person.* His love is the fountain of His work and operations.

1. Renewing. 2. Comforting. 3. Sealing. 4. Grieving at our sins. 5. Helping our infirmities. 6. Shedding abroad the love of God. 7. Making intercession for us. All these flow from love, as sevenfold rays from pure white light.

First group: Jud. iii. 10, vi. 34. In these verses notice, the power of the Spirit enabling

His chosen instruments for work or warfare seems the leading idea. For our comfort in sense of weakness link with 1 Cor. xii., "Same Spirit" seven times. Apply this to reading of or observing the work of the Spirit in others. Jud. vi. 34; 1 Chron. xii. 18; clothed in "glorious apparel" (Isa. lxiii. 1), denoting the gifts and graces of the Holy Spirit, clothing outwardly as well as filling inwardly. Connect with the prayer, "Endue them with innocency of life"; clothe, invest, array.

Second group: 1 Sam. x. 6, 10; xvi. 14. Temporary influences of the Spirit.

Third group: Ps. li. 11, 12; cxxxix. 7; cxliii. 10. Group how you will, so comprehensive.

i. See three titles of the Spirit: 1. Holy, as He is in Himself. 2. Good or loving, as He is *towards* us. 3. Free, the essence of His work in us. 2 Cor. iii. 17: "glorious liberty."

ii. (1) Deity and omnipresence. (2) Actual possession and possible loss. (3) Upholding. (4) Loving and leading.

Ps. li. 11: "Take not Thy Holy Spirit from me"; contrast with Hag. ii. 5. Key to the difficulty. There may be (1) influence of the Spirit upon the mind, (2) *conscious* presence of the Spirit; and both these may be withdrawn. But

the promised or the covenanted gift of the Spirit
"remaineth." If we have taken hold of the
"covenant," *all* covenanted blessings are ours,
"everlasting" as the covenant itself (Luke x. 42).
Solemn to think of the passing impulses of the
Spirit, but joyful to know that His real work
abideth.

The promise in Hag. ii. 5 has a special
Association connection (see context, ver. 4),
"work," building of the spiritual temple; we
are called to bring the stones, the precept and
the promise for us. If we are *not* working, not
obeying the precept, we lose our claim to the
promise; how many promises are lost thus.

Fourth group: 1 Chron. xxviii. 19, compare
ver. 12, Spirit and Jehovah; hence Deity of
the Spirit.

In writing, whether for the press or letters,
write for God, and He will teach ourselves by
it. I would advise *written* preparation for Sun-
day school or Bible-class teaching.

Fifth group: 2 Chron. xv. 1, xx. 14, xxiv. 20.
Three instances typical of *our* work. 1. Azariah,
calling to those who are "without God" to turn
to Him, leading them to *prayer*. 2. Jahaziel,
encouraging and strengthening those who *are*
on the Lord's side, leading them to *praise*. 3.

Zechariah, witnessing against sin and departure from God; compare Neh. ix. 30.

What account have we to give of our Young Women's Christian Association membership under these three points?

NOTES OF F. R. H.'S ADDRESS TO Y. W. C. A. AT SWANSEA, THURSDAY, APRIL 17, 1879.

Hosea iii. 1–3. One of the most precious double promises of the Bible. Is it for us? See who it is for—if we answer to the description. The question need never be, are we *good* enough, but are we *bad* enough, for claiming the promise.

I. Our personal position.

1. Beloved, yet faithless. (Isa. lxiii. 7–10.) The love of the Lord (Mal. i. 2; 1 John iv. 10; Jer. xxxi. 3; John xiii. 1). "Yet" treacherous, and He knew it (Isa. xlviii. 8). "Who look to other gods" (Isa. xxvi. 13). Who "love flagons of wine," *i.e.* earthly joys, craving, etc. Guilty under the first command (Matt. xxii. 37). Does this describe us? or

do we remember His love "more than wine" (Cant. 1. 4)?

2. *"Bought"* (ver. 2). "*So* I bought her," because no other way would do. The faithless one must be made His own by right. (1 Cor. vi. 19, 20.) "Redeemed with the precious blood of Christ" (1 Pet. 1. 19). There is the force of the "*so,*" by Thine agony and bloody sweat, by Thy cross and passion (Isa. liii. 3); *so* He bought her.

Another view of "so" is just contrary to what we should have expected, "let him alone (Hos. iv. 17). "And I said after she had done all these things, Turn thou unto me" (Jer. iii. 7).

"Bought her *to Me.*" Boaz purchased Ruth to be His wife (Ruth iv. 8, 10); only money there, here blood. What intensity of desire is implied! How Jesus must have *wanted* us. "In His *love* and in His pity He redeemed."

II. The Lord's personal covenant with us.

1. "Thou shalt abide for Me." "Shalt" has a fourfold meaning: (1) *Purpose* (Ps. iv. 3: 2 Tim. iv. 18; Isa. xliii. 21; Rom. xi. 4). Now: "seemeth it but a small thing unto you, that the God of Israel hath separated you from the congregation of Israel, to bring you near to Him-

self?" (Num. xvi. 9.) (2) *Command.* *"Shalt,"*
"for," "in," "with me." (3) *Promise* (Ps. xc. 1).
Shall abide; compare "ye shall abide in Him"
(1 John ii. 27). Christ undertakes our part,
because we *cannot* (Zech. ix. 7). And the new
covenant was established (Heb. viii. 8–10).
Won't you trust Him to do this (Isa. xxxviii. 14)?
(4) *Resolve* (Ps. lxxx. 17, 18, with Jude 24).

"Many days"; compare Matt. xxviii. 20, *i.e.*
"all the days," and Exod. xxi. 6.

"So will I also be for thee." In the past
(Gal. ii. 20), but see the *present*; *e.g.* a mother
"lives for" her child, thinking, caring, watch-
ing, providing, managing, directing, *cherisheth.*
" *So* will I also be for thee," in every detail; *e.g.*
Rom. viii. 31, Ps. lvi. 9.

Who then is willing to enter this full, blessed,
complete covenant? Personal, *"with me"* (2
Sam. xxiii. 5; Eccles. iii. 14), *Now,* " come,"
etc. (Jer. l. 5.)

"If you are not *for* Him, you are *against,"*
(Luke xi. 23,) your side against God, God's
side "against thee" (Ezek. xxxv. 3). But take
a contrasted glimpse; if you are willing to
be *"for Him,"* you have the King's own
answer, now, "Behold, I am for you" (Ezek.
xxxvi. 9; Hos. ii. 19, 20; Isa. xliv. 5).

MISCELLANEOUS PAPERS.

SICKNESS FROM GOD'S HAND.

(Written after reading a contrary statement).

I. DIRECT TESTIMONY FROM SCRIPTURE.

Lev. xxvi. 16: In threatening consumption and the burning ague, God says, "I also will do this unto you."

Deut. vii. 15: "*The Lord* . . . will put none of the evil diseases of Egypt . . . upon thee; but will lay them upon all them that hate thee."

Deut. xxviii. 27: "*The Lord* will smite thee with the botch of Egypt," etc. Ver. 35: "*The Lord* shall smite thee in the legs and in the knees," etc. Ver. 59–61: "Then *the Lord* will make thy plagues wonderful, . . . sore sicknesses, and of long continuance, moreover *He* will bring upon thee all the diseases of Egypt, . . . also every sickness and every plague . . . them will *the Lord* bring upon thee."

2. Sam. xii. 15: "*The Lord* struck the child, and it was very sick."

2. Chron. xxi. 18: "*The Lord* smote Him in his bowels with an incurable disease."

"And the *Lord* smote the king so that he was a leper unto the day of his death" (2 Kings xv. 5).

Ps. xxxii. 4: "For day and night *Thy* hand was heavy upon me." It is an evident description of fever.

Ps. xxxviii. 2: "*Thine* arrows stick fast in me, *Thy* hand presseth me sore." The context again shows this to have been severe sickness.

Ps. xxxix. 10; "Remove *Thy* stroke away from me; I am consumed by the blow of *Thine* hand." The consuming in this and next verse again describes the normal effect of sickness.

Isa. xxxviii. 15: "HIMSELF *hath done it.*" This needs no comment, enough if it stood alone in the Bible!

Micah vi. 13: "Therefore also will *I* make thee sick in smiting thee."

Acts xii. 23: "The angel of *the Lord* smote him." (Herod.)

II. INDIRECT TESTIMONY.

Ps. xli. 3: "*Thou* wilt make all his bed in his sickness." Does not this tender, sympathetic, and continuous care in sickness militate against the idea that sickness is from Satan, and therefore "not to be remained under!"

Ps. cxxi. 7: "*The Lord* shall preserve thee from *all evil.*"

I will put the argument from this into two syllogisms.

(1) What is of Satan must be evil. God's people are preserved from *all evil.* *Therefore,* God's people are preserved from whatever is of Satan.

(2) God's people are preserved from whatever is of Satan. They are not preserved from sickness. *Therefore,* sickness is not of Satan.

2 Sam. xxiv. 14. David expressly says that in accepting the pestilence he is falling into the hand of *the Lord.* "And *the Lord* sent a pestilence upon Israel," etc.

Ps. lxxxviii. 3, 4, 6. Ver. 3, 4, apparently imply sickness: "nigh unto the grave," "no strength"; but David follows it with "*Thou* hast laid me in the lowest pit, in darkness, in the deeps."

I suppose we all agree, and often tell others, that "*all* things," in Rom. viii. 28, really means "ALL things," sickness included; if we do, must we not equally say that in 2 Cor. v. 18 "*all* things" really means ALL things, sickness included !

"Chastening," so far as I can recollect, is

always spoken of as the act of God. But in Job xxxiii. 19 sickness is distinctly spoken of and stated to be chastening, *ergo*, from God. Also equally distinctly in Ps. cxviii. 18, from God.

(In passing, what a wonderful parallel that passage, Job xxxiii. 19–28, has with James v. 14–16.)

Luke ix. 1: *Christ* gave them power and authority over all devils, *and* to cure diseases, *i.e. two separate* things.

There are several similar passages. The way in which sickness is mentioned four times in Matthew xxv. does not seem to harmonise with the Satanic theory, though I cannot formulate it.

Similarly the mention in John xi. 4.—Leprosy is the typical sickness, and the one of all others which one would *expect* to be referred to Satan, and the one over which Christ especially displayed His power; but so far as I recollect, it is never once spoken of in connection with the devil, but always inferentially as from *God Himself*, this being expressly stated in 2 Kings xv. 5, already quoted. St. Paul would hardly have left Trophinus at Miletum sick, and spoken so very calmly of the fact, if he had believed *that* sickness to be from Satan, and "not to be remained under."

That Satan may be permitted in special cases to be the direct instrument of sickness, *e.g.* Job, also the woman of Samaria (Luke xiii. 11), is a *very* different thing, and seems as clear as that he is not the usual and normal instrument. The *mass* of instances on the other side, and the plainest Bible statements, surely preclude this.

June 2, 1878.   F. R. H.

ARE *ALL* THE CHILDREN OF GOD?*

No text shows the affirmative. On the other hand:

I. It is distinctly stated that some are *not* the children of God. "They which are the children of the flesh, these are not the children of God" (Rom. ix. 8). "In this the children of God are manifest, and the children of the devil; whosoever doeth not righteousness is not of God, neither he that loveth not his brother" (1 John iii. 10; John viii. 41, 42, 44).

* Written after F. R. H.'s return from church, where *all* the congregation were addressed as being the children of God.

II. Distinct conditions are annexed to being, or becoming, the children of God, which are manifestly not fulfilled by all.

First condition. *Believing* on the name of Christ and receiving Him. "But as many as received Him, to them gave He power to become the sons of God, even to them that believe on His name" (John i. 12). Also Gal. iii. 26.

Second condition. *Love* to the Lord Jesus Christ. "Jesus said unto them, If God were your Father ye would love Me" (John viii. 42).

Third condition. *Being led* by the Spirit. "For as many as are led by the Spirit of God, they are the sons of God" (Rom. viii. 14).

III. The children of God are constantly mentioned in contradistinction to others who are described as the children of a different father or power. See Rom. ix. 8; 1 John iii. 10; Matt. xiii. 38; Eph. ii. 2, 3, 5, 6; Luke xvi. 8; and many other passages. Observe that when St. Paul called Elymas "child of the devil" (Acts xiii. 10), it is expressly said in ver. 9 that Paul was "filled with the Holy Ghost." I have looked out (with concordance) every place where "children" or "sons of God" occurs, and am struck with two facts.

1. That, even when not expressly stated to apply only to some and not to all, the same is *implied* in every case; *e. g.*, Matt. v. 44, 45, "Love your enemies, bless them that curse you, do good to them that hate you, and pray for them which despitefully use you and persecute you; *That ye may* be the children of your Father which is in heaven," *not* "because" ye *are!*

2. That baptism is never once said to be the means of adoption, or of being or becoming, the children of God.

SIX ILLUSTRATIONS OF THE UNITY IN DIVERSITY OF THE HOLY SCRIPTURES.

(1) The system of typical persons, places, things, and events, all converging in the Person and offices of Christ.

(2) The steadily increasing light of prophecy, from the Seed (Gen. iii. 15) to the Sun (Mal. iv. 2).

(3) The gradual revelation of God Himself throughout the whole Old Testament, till Christ came, "God manifest in the flesh," and then the unfolding of that revelation throughout the New.

(4) The striking unity of conception in the allusions to creation in Job, Psalms, Proverbs, Ecclesiastes, and the prophets.

(5) The startling *contrasts* between Ecclesiastes and the Song of Solomon, suggesting evident design in their inspiration and juxtaposition.

(6) The connection of the Book of Proverbs with the *history* of the Old Testament and the *morality* of the New.

All of these (and many others) would be interesting to work out thoroughly.   I take one only as a specimen—the last named.

I. The Book of Proverbs seems to be an epitome of the lessons to be learnt from the whole of Scripture history; or the history as a volume of illustrations of the Proverbs.   Taking a single book (chosen haphazard), the Second of Chronicles, we find the following parallels.   (This list is by no means exhaustive.)

2 Chronicles.	Proverbs.	2 Chronicles.	Proverbs.
i. 10 compare	iv. 5–7.	x. 6–13 compare	xxix. 9.
i. 12 "	iii. 16.	xi. 1–4 "	xxi. 30.
ii. 3 "	xxvii. 10.	xiv. 11 "	xviii. 10.
vi. 30 "	xv. 11.	xvi. 7–8 "	xxix. 25.
ix. 2 "	xx. 5.	xviii. 7 "	xxix. 10.
x. 6 "	xxvii. 10.	xx. 35 "	xxii. 24, 25.
x. 7 "	xv. 1.	xx. 37 "	xiii. 20.

2 Chronicles.	Proverbs.		2 Chronicles.	Proverbs.
xxiii. 13 compare	xi. 10.		xxix. 36 compare	xvi. 1.
xxiv. 17, 18 "	xxix. 12.		xxx. 9-11 "	xxviii. 13.
xxiv. 22 "	xvii. 13.		xxx. 26 "	xxix. 2.
xxv. 9 "	x. 22.		xxxii. 8 "	xii. 25.
xxvi. 16 "	{ xxix. 23. / xvi. 18. }		xxxii. 31 "	xvii. 3.
			xxxiv. 3 "	viii. 17.
xxviii. 15 "	xxv. 21.		xxxvi. 5, 9, 11 "	xxviii. 2.

II. The morality of the Proverbs is identical with that of the New Testament. The precepts of the former *generally* occur as statements in the latter, and *vice versa; e. g.:*

Prov. iii. 9	compare	1 Cor. xvi. 2.
iii. 28	"	Matt. v. 42.
viii. 13	"	Rom. xii. 9.
x. 12	"	1 Pet. iv. 8.
xi. 12	"	Rom. xii. 16.
xii. 20	"	Matt. v. 9.
xiv. 17, 29	"	James i. 19.
xviii. 12	"	James iv. 10.
xix. 11	"	Matt. xviii. 22.
xx. 21	"	1 Tim. vi. 9-11.
xxi. 4	"	Rom. xiv. 23.
xxiv. 29	"	1 Pet. iii. 9.
xxviii. 21	"	James ii. 1 (& *e. g.* Jude 16).

III. *Every* book in the New Testament has some parallel in Proverbs, some chapters (*e. g.* Rom. xii., James iv.) having parallels with nearly every verse.

Matt. v. 8	compare	Proverbs xxii. 11.
Mark xii. 33	"	xxi. 3.
Luke xii. 24, 27	"	vi. 6.
John xii. 26	"	xxvii. 18.
Acts v. 1–8	"	xix. 5, 9.
Rom. xii. 16	"	iii. 7.
1 Cor. xv. 33	"	xxii. 24, 25.
2 Cor. ix. 6	"	xi. 24, 25.
Gal. vi. 7–9	"	xi. 18, xxii. 8.
Eph. iv. 31	"	iv. 24.
Phil. iii. 13, 14	"	iv. 25.
Col. i. 9, 11	"	xxiv. 5.
1 Thess. v. 15	"	xx. 22.
2 Thess. iii. 11, 12	"	xiv. 23.
1 Tim. vi. 17	"	xi. 28.
2 Tim. iii. 15	"	xxii. 6.
Tit. i. 13	"	xv. 32.
Philem. 20	"	xii. 20.
Heb. iv. 13	"	xv. 11.
James i. 5	"	iv. 7.
1 Pet. iii. 15	"	xxii. 21.
2 Pet. iii. 15, } Gal. ii. 11 }	"	xxviii. 23.
1 John iii. 22	"	xv. 29.
2 John 11	"	xvii. 15.
3 John 10	"	x. 8, 10.
Jude 10	"	iv. 19.
Rev. iii. 19	"	iii. 11, 12.

INTERNAL EVIDENCE OF THE PROBABILITY THAT ST. PAUL WROTE THE EPISTLE TO THE HEBREWS.

I. Similarity of *style* with his other epistles.

1. The order of: first doctrine (chap. i. to xi.), then practice (chaps. xii., xiii.).

2. His continuous argument, yet parenthetical idiosyncrasy; *e. g.*, chap. iii. 7–11, iv. 7–10.

3. His manner of Old Testament quotations, resembling especially in this the Epistle to the Romans.

4. His way of drawing inferences from single words (as in Gal. iii. 16); *e. g.*, "under" (Heb. ii. 8), "new" (viii. 13), "yet once more" (xii. 27).

5. His use of a postscript. Adaptation to those to whom he wrote. We could have been sure this epistle was *meant* for the Hebrews, just as we see the adaptation of the Romans.

II. Similarity as to favorite *words; e. g.* (1) "therefore" and "wherefore," his constant link between doctrine and practice. (2) His courteous "I beseech." (3) Christ as the "Son." (4) "Remember." (5) "Promise," etc., etc.

III. Similarity ("in diversity") of *topic:* (1)

Faith; (2) Submission to authority, doing good
to others, and other practical points.

IV. Miscellaneous evidence.

1. Negative.

(*a*) It was *not* by one of the twelve, and probably not by one who had personally "heard Him"
while on earth.   See Heb. ii. 3.

(*b*) It was apparently not by one who himself
held definite rule or office in any church (chap.
xiii. 7, 17).

(*c*) It was not by an obscure individual who
required introduction, or apology, or creden-
tials.

2. Positive.

(*a*) It was written by one who had been in
bonds (Heb. x. 34); (*b*) and who had been
helped by those to whom he wrote (Phil. iv. 14);
(*c*) who had apparently had experience of re-
proach (chap. xiii. 13), and of "wanderings"
(chap. xiii. 14); (*d*) who was intimately ac-
quainted with Jewish laws and customs; (*e*) who
had written longer epistles than this (chap. xiii.
22); (*f*) who was *in* Italy but only as sojourner
(chap xiii. 19, "restored to you"); (*g*) who was
intimate with Timothy, using the term "brother,"
St. Paul's usual epithet in speaking *of* him (N. B.
he speaks *to* him as "son"); (*h*) who rejoiced

to acknowledge good in others (chap. vi. 9), yet was faithful in reproof (chap. v. 12); (*i*) who seemed to feel and bear "the care of all the churches" (2 Cor. xi. 28); (*j*) who acknowledges God's grace in himself (Acts xxiii. 1, and Heb. xiii. 18).

V. Coincidences between the 13th chapter and the other Pauline epistles (not already mentioned).

Heb. xiii. 1	1 Thess. iv. 9.
2	Rom. xii. 13.
3	Philem. 1; Eph. iii. 1; Col. iv. 18.
4	Eph. v. 23–32.
5	1 Tim. vi. 9–11.
— 2nd clause	1 Tim. vi. 6–8; Phil. iv. 11.
— 3rd clause	Rom. viii. 35, 38, 39.
6	2 Tim. iv. 17, 18.
7	1 Thess. v. 12.
— 2nd clause	1 Cor. xi. 1.
8	1 Cor. ii. 2.
9	2 Tim. iv. 3; 1 Tim. iv. 16.
— 2nd clause	2 Thess. ii. 17.
— 3rd clause	Rom. xiv.
12	1 Cor. i. 30.
13	2 Cor. vi. 17.
14	2 Cor. v. 1; Phil. iii. 20.
15	Eph. v. 20.
—2nd cl. margin	Rom. x. 9, 10.
16	Rom. xii. 13; Gal. vi. 10.

Heb. xiii. 16 2nd clause	.	Phil. iv. 18.
17		1 Thess. v. 12.
— 2nd clause	.	1 Cor. xvi. 16.
— last clause	.	1 Thess. ii. 19, 20.
18		2 Cor. i. 11.
— 2nd clause	.	2 Cor. i. 12; 2 Tim. i. 3.
— 3rd clause	.	{ 2 Thess. iii. 8, 9; Rom. xii. 17.
19	.	{ Rom. i. 10; and xv. 30–32. Philem. 22.
20, 21 . . .	.	{ 1 Thess. v. 23; 2 Thess. ii. 16.
20, 1st clause	.	{ Rom. xv. 33, xvi. 20; Phil. iv. 9.
— 2nd clause	.	Rom. viii. 11; 1 Cor. vi. 14.
21	.	{ Col. i. 10; Phil. ii. 13. Eph. ii. 10, i. 19, iii. 13.
22		Philem. 9.
— 2nd clause	.	Gal. vi. 11.
23		2 Tim. iv. 21.

VI. Coincidences between this Epistle and St. Paul's speeches in Acts. It seems remarkable that these occur most in the *later* speeches, those which are nearest to the date of the Epistle.

P. S.—I have only glanced at the "Acts" coincidences, and have not yet worked them out.

CPSIA information can be obtained
at www.ICGtesting.com
Printed in the USA
BVHW042318180121
598084BV00005B/170